# ART & ARCHITECTURE
# BIBLIOGRAPHIES, I

Fig. 1. Title page of James Logan's copy of the Amsterdam 1649 edition of Vitruvius' *Architectura* (courtesy: Library Company of Philadelphia).

# A LIST OF
# ARCHITECTURAL BOOKS
# AVAILABLE IN AMERICA
# BEFORE
# THE REVOLUTION

## by

# HELEN PARK

new edition, revised and enlarged
with a foreword by

ADOLF K. PLACZEK

Hennessey & Ingalls, Inc.
Los Angeles        1973

The original version of this checklist was published as an article in the *Journal of the Society of Architectural Historians* (Vol. XX, October 1961) and is used as the basis of this book by permission of the Society.

Z
5941
.P35
1973

Copyright © 1961 by the Society of Architectural Historians. New material copyright © 1973 by Helen Park. All rights reserved. Printed in the United States of America.

ISBN Number: 0-912158-21-2
LC Number: 76-189461

Library
UNIVERSITY OF MIAMI

*to my husband*

# CONTENTS

# FOREWORD

## by Adolf K. Placzek

The *List of Architectural Books Available in America before the Revolution* by Helen Park, or the "Park List" as it is often called, has by now become one of the basic bibliographic tools for the student of American architectural history, even though it could not easily be obtained because it was published in the pages of a journal (*Journal of the Society of Architectural Historians*, v. 20, no. 3, October 1961). This new edition in book form, with substantial additions and revisions by the author, will therefore be welcomed by a great number of scholars and will assure the wide distribution which this important work deserves.

What does the "Park List" tell us? First of all, the stylistic, pictorial and structural sources of much of colonial architecture. In many cases, it even points the way to the exact plate from which a decorative motif or building detail was taken. It leads us to certain books (106 in all); and in reverse, it eliminates a great many others which—according to Mrs. Park's painstaking research—were plainly *not* available on the North American continent. The relatively small number of the architectural books which were available, incidentally, is one of the surprising facts the list reveals.

The list also tells us, of course, quite a good deal about the cultural scene in eighteenth-century America. There is, expectedly but re-confirmed, the predominance of the English connection. Of the 106 books, only 8 do not carry a British imprint (and four of these were to be found only at Harvard College). None of the great French source books of design—neither Androuet Du Cerceau nor Marot, neither Blondel nor Mariette—are included in the list. It can therefore be assumed that they were unknown to the colonial builders. The absence of any original Italian Alberti is conspicuous, as is the paucity of Vignolas. Even the great English Serlio of 1611 is not represented. The taste, then, was not simply British, but Palladian-British, that is, in the academic classicist mold of the Earl of Burlington and his adherents Colen Campbell, Giacomo Leoni, Robert Morris, William Kent—all names appearing on the Park List.

What emerges further from the list is the overwhelmingly practical nature of the needs of America's eighteenth-century builders. These men—although their skill, their refinement and their aesthetic sense must never be underestimated—were not trained architects as were their English counterparts. The first colonial architect was Peter Harrison (1716-1775), who arrived in New England in 1739 having already been professionally trained in England; he was a great bearer of architectural books too. But what the men who built America's lovely and sturdy colonial structures needed most were handbooks, builders' handbooks; the works of Langley (11 titles), Pain (2 titles), Swan (4 titles), Salmon (4 titles) and Halfpenny (12 titles!) abound on Mrs. Park's list. In fact, no English handbook author is missing. When these early builders reached for sophistication, they turned to Isaac Ware and James Gibbs;

for strict Palladian theory, obviously to Robert Morris (4 titles). And they used these books thoroughly. Many of the volumes preserved are conspicuously worn, stained and foxed. They were obviously carried in the breeches pockets of men on the job—used, even on rainy days, even with dirty hands. They became "collector's items" much later.

How did American architectural literature develop after Mrs. Park's cut-off date? What are the bibliographic sources documenting the next phases? I would refer the reader above all to Henry-Russell Hitchcock's *American Architectural Books* (1946, reprinted 1962) which lists all architectural titles published *in* America before 1895. A close comparison of the Hitchcock and Park bibliographies is fruitful. It will be apparent that even after the start of the American revolution the English architectural influence was total. The first American architectural imprint was Abraham Swan's *The British Architect* (1775), a re-issue of no. 9 on Mrs. Park's list; the second was John Norman's *Town and Country Builder's Assistant* (1786), also an Englishman's work; the third was William Pain's *The Practical Builder* (1792), a re-issue of a London book of 1774; two more William Pain titles, *The Builder's Pocket Treasure* (1794)—see Mrs. Park's no. 64—and *The Practical Carpenter* (1796) followed. Not until 1797 was there an American architectural book which was also authored by an American—Asher Benjamin's *The Country Builder's Assistant.* A new era of American architectural book publishing dates from that milestone book. Thereafter, the printed sources soon became numerous and more easily available. Several American authors followed, Owen Biddle and John Haviland among the first. The French and Italian books began to arrive. A good example of what the architectural library of a really sophisticated architect after the Revolution would contain is the list of architectural books owned by Thomas Jefferson, as reproduced in Fiske Kimball's *Thomas Jefferson, Architect* (1916, reprinted 1968). He owned many of the great French and Italian works on architecture in the grand style, but only two practical English handbooks (by Halfpenny and Langley respectively). The architectural book holdings of the U.S. were well on their way to the enormous outpouring of the next century, and to the more than 40,000 specifically architectural titles listed in the printed catalogue of the Avery Architectural Library (1968).

But, in colonial America, it all began on a small scale, a few books used again and again to build houses, schools, barns, meeting places and churches in small communities on the edge of the wilderness, many of them exquisitely scaled, sited and detailed. There are only 106 titles, and judging from the research of the last ten years, it appears unlikely that many new ones will be unearthed. The "Park List," as it stands, seems pretty definitive. It is good to have it in print again.

Adolf K. Placzek
February 1972                              Avery Librarian

# PREFACE

**The opportunity** for correction and moderate expansion provided by a new edition of this pre-Revolutionary American architectural bibliography proved irresistible. A thorough search of book lists now so readily available in the Evans microprint series as well as a search of manuscript and printed material at the American Antiquarian Society, the Massachusetts Historical Society, the libraries of Columbia University, and the Library Company of Philadelphia have produced an additional nineteen titles.

The most satisfactory result has been the emergence of the background of colonial building in mathematics, geometry, drawing, surveying, and measuring books of all kinds which appear again and again. Even the earliest lists, disappointingly few and incomplete, include basic mathematical texts. To compute, to measure, to cut a straight timber for a house, to place a house desirably on a piece of land whose boundaries and outlook you understood, could all be done with information available in illustrated texts, widely owned and used. An interested owner could direct the building operations himself; his indentured servants were frequently bricklayers or carpenters.

The examination of two libraries, that of Samuel Johnson and his son William Samuel Johnson, 1st and 3rd presidents of King's College (Columbia University), and of Mather Byles, a grandson of Increase Mather, who died in Boston in 1788, demonstrate the presence of measuring books in general libraries. Byles owned Darling's *Carpenters Rule Made Easie,* an early manual printed by the Leybourns who published a number of early mathematical, surveying, and architectural books. Byles also owned Foster's *Art of Measuring,* another seventeenth-century imprint which, it is fair to speculate, he inherited from his grandfather. In the Johnson library at Columbia, two books, signed and dated by William Samuel Johnson in 1758, demonstrate the mathematical background to building in books published in the eighteenth century: Hawney's *Compleat Measurer,* which went through twelve editions between 1717 and 1766, and William Salmon's *London and Country Builder's Vade Mecum: or the Complete and Universal Estimator.*

Venterus Mandey's *Marrow of Measuring* (first edition 1682) was advertised in Boston in 1734, as was Seth Partridge's *Description and Use of an Instrument Called the Double Scale of Proportion*, first published in 1671. In 1772, Cox and Berry in Boston were advertising a work by Thomas Miles, Surveyor, *The Concise Practical Measurer; or, a Plain Guide to Gentlemen and Builders* (a second edition in 1740). John Crunden, an author of the 1760's, noted that he wanted to make his designs clear to "gentlemen and architects."

The cooperation of the staffs of the Huntington Library and the Avery Library in the use of their facilities is gratefully acknowledged. Edition dates reflect the careful cooperation of librarians all over the country, but particularly those at Colonial Williamsburg, Winterthur, the Virginia Historical Society and the Boston Athenaeum. Dr. Placzek's interest has been unflagging.

The essay which accompanied original publication of the list has been corrected in light of later information. The statistics on usage have always been troublesome. Scholars like Abbot Cummings of the Society for the Preseveration of New England Antiquities will be relieved to find a more predictable source such as Salmon's *Palladio Londinensis* topping the list in number of references. His view that we were not getting at the early sources is reinforced by the early publications which appear in the Byles and Johnson libraries.

The
First Book of Architecture by
ANDREA PALLADIO
translated out of Italian w.th diuerse
other designes necessary to the art
of well building by
Godfrey Richards

And are to be sold at his shop at the signe of the Peacock
in Cornhil neere the old Exchange London :
John Chantry sculp.

Fig. 2. Title page, Richards' translation of Palladio, *The First Book of Architecture*, London, 1663 (courtesy: Avery Library).

# INTRODUCTION

**All the Arts** in England were enlivened with a resurgence of interest and an influx of new talent under the patronage of Charles II after the long interruption of Puritan government. This artistic revival included a gradual renewal of architectural classicism introduced to England by Inigo Jones and interrupted by the hiatus in building under the Commonwealth. Spurred in London by the rebuilding which followed the Great Fire of 1666, the movement spread from the court throughout the British Empire by means of architectural handbooks. How-to-do-it books were a phenomenon of the age of reason when measurable proportion was the canon of

1

taste. In building, they supplemented books of plans and elevations and were the instruments for spreading Palladian doctrine to the provinces and colonies.

The first how-to-do-it guide to the practical arts appeared in 1670, Joseph Moxon's *Mechanick Exercises,* a series of pamphlets which included three on house carpentry. They must have made their way to the American colonies, but no identifiable reference has been found. One plate showed a narrow three-story, three-bayed house in elevation. A glossary of terms was included, a useful feature of many later manuals.

The earliest handbook in this revised list is John Darling's *Carpenter's Rule Made Easie*, published in 1658 and owned by Mather Byles of Boston. In 1663 Godfrey Richards published a translation of the first book of Palladio's *Quattro libri dell'architettura*, and included a supplement on doors and windows by the French architect Pierre Le Muet. Richards' handbook is the earliest Palladian source in English for which American colonial references have been found. Richards' translation went into a second edition in 1668, two years after the Great Fire. The preface notes this as an opportune moment to reissue Palladio's requirements for "Accommodation, Handsomeness and Lastingness" when "a new and great City is to be built," and looks forward to "a second happy restoration, inferiour only to that of his Majesties Person and Government."

Such translations or native English instructions continued to appear at intervals until a fresh impetus was provided in 1715 by the Earl of Burlington, who returned from Italy in that year to sponsor the first major design book of English Palladianism, Colen Campbell's *Vitruvius Britannicus,* a monumental three-volume folio with plates of "classical" buildings by Jones, Webb, Wren, Vanbrugh, and Campbell himself. Its preface stated the Palladian credo:

> With [Palladio] the great manner and exquisite Taste of Building is lost; for the *Italians* can no more now relish the Antique Simplicity, but are entirely employed in capricious Ornaments, which must at last end in the *Gothick.* . . . How affected and licentious are the Works of *Bernini*, and *Fontana*? How wildly extravagant are the Designs of *Boromini*, who has endeavour'd to debauch mankind with his odd and chimerical Beauties, where the Parts are without Proportion, Solids without their true Bearing, Heaps of Materials without Strength, excessive Ornament without Grace, and the whole without Symmetry?

Campbell's plates are equally explicit in illustrating the attenuation of Inigo Jones' vigorous assimilation of Italian Renaissance classicism in the Banqueting Hall at Whitehall into the flattened correctness of Campbell's house for the Duke of Argyll. For the next sixty years design books and handbooks giving plans and directions for constructing Palladian buildings flooded the market, augmented by handbooks with specifications for counter-Palladian embellishments in the rococo, Chinese, and ancient tastes.

References to one hundred and six of these books have been found in pre-Revolutionary American records. Only one documented seventeenth century reference was found. The early books in the Mather Byles library may have been owned by his grandfather Increase Mather, part of whose library he inherited. But there is no complete record of the family's seventeenth century libraries. About half of the identified books were builders' manuals, with the detailed instructions for achieving a "just proportion" in building upon which promulgation of Palladian doctrine depended. Only a few references were found to big prestige books like Campbell's; those with the most references are the ones aimed at the lowest common denominator, or the "meanest" intelligence in eighteenth-century phraseology. The references were found in the catalogues of institutional libraries, in book-sellers' catalogues, in newspaper advertisements, and in individual inventories. Thirty-nine titles appear in institutional lists, of which twenty-five do not appear in advertisements. Twenty-four appear uniquely in private inventories. Sixty-seven were advertised, but only four before 1750.

Except for the William Byrd collection at Westover, only four certain references to architectural books in America before 1730 were found: to Fréart's *Parallel of the Ancient Architecture with the Modern* in the Samuel Lee library catalogued by Boston bookseller Duncan Campbell in 1693 (the only seventeenth century reference in this list); to John James' translation of Claude Perrault's *Treatise of the Five Orders in Architecture* in the Harvard College Library catalogue of 1723, listed with Wotton's *Elements*; and to a handbook, John Barker's *The Measurer's Guide* in the Bray library of Christ Church in Philadelphia, a library which must have arrived about 1700, according to Edwin Wolf II. For the years 1730 through 1750, references to four manuals advertised in Boston and Philadelphia were found, and also references to eight titles (and ten books) in institutional libraries, five in the Library Company of Philadelphia, three in the Redwood Library in Newport, and two at Yale.

Geographically, the information covers five major colonial cities, Boston, Newport, New York, Philadelphia, and Charleston, with one catalogue of books sold by Benedict Arnold in New Haven probably in 1765. All that have survived of pre-Revolutionary American university library catalogues and seven private libraries are included and generally fall within this geographic distribution. Pre-Revolutionary catalogues exist only for Harvard, Yale, and Princeton, although William and Mary, King's College (Columbia), the University of Pennsylvania, Brown, Rutgers, and Dartmouth were established in the Colonial period. Princeton's only colonial catalogue is dated 1760, and no architectural books were listed. Yale had only two in 1741, as did Harvard until 1765 when several volumes of Italian architectural theory were added. The private libraries are those of the builder Thomas Dawes of Boston, the architects Peter Harrison of Newport and William Buckland of Annapolis, James Logan of Philadelphia (secretary to William Penn and chief justice of the Supreme Court of Pennsylvania), William Byrd, the owner of Westover in Virginia, Mather Byles, a grandson of Increase Mather who inherited some of his grandfather's books, and William Samuel Johnson, the third president of Columbia University, whose library included signed and dated books that fall within the scope of this study.

Only books which specifically apply to the art of building have been listed. Books of antiquities have been excluded, although they of course underlie the architectural handbooks of the neoclassical movement. They were significantly present at Harvard in 1765 and at the Library Company of

Philadelphia in 1770. Potter's *Antiquities of Greece* appears as early as 1755 in the New York catalogue of bookseller Garrett Noel and, along with Kennett's *Antiquities of Rome*, in John Mein's Boston circulating library in 1765. Both were widely owned privately. Books of perspective have been included when they are identifiably oriented toward architecture.

A quantity of unproductive material has been examined. No architectural books appear in the inventory, now in the Connecticut State Library in Hartford, of another grandson of Increase Mather, Warham Mather, who died in New Haven in 1745. There are no books at all listed in the manuscript inventories of the estates of Gerard Beekman, John Beekman, Richard Stillwell, and Anna Hooglandt, all of whom died in New York in the years 1726-1774, and whose inventories are now in the New York Public Library. Adolph Philipse, who died in New York in 1749, owned "a parcel of books" but, as so often happened, they were not itemized. Swem's encyclopaedic *Virginia Historical Index* refers to only four architectural books in the period covered by this study. One of these, in the library of Colonel John Carter (died 1690) of Lancaster County, has not been identified.[1] A "guide for builders" listed in the inventory of Colonel Maximilian Boush, who died in Princess Anne County in 1728, may be Keay's *Practical Measurer, or Plain Guide to Gentlemen and*

---

1. *William and Mary Quarterly,* series 1, VIII, No. 1 (1899), 18. A great many inventories have been printed in this quarterly, in the *Virginia Magazine of History and Biography, Tyler's Quarterly,* etc., indexed in Earl Gregg Swem, *Virginia Historical Index.*

*Builders* (number 34), but we cannot be sure.[2] Two others, in the library of Councillor Robert Carter of Nomini Hall, Westmoreland County, *Palladio Londinensis* and *Builder's Treasure of Designs* (probably Batty Langley's), were probably there before 1776, but they have not been included because this study is limited to recorded references before the outbreak of the Revolution.[3] A fifth reference, to a "Vad. Mecum" in the library of Colonel John Waller, who died in Spotsylvania County in 1755, may of course be to Salmon's *London and Country Builder's Vade Mecum*, but again we do not know.[4] It seems clear, however, that quite early there was a scattering of architectural books in the colonies. A copy of Vitruvius, again the 1649 Amsterdam edition, in the Winthrop library presented to the Massachusetts Historical Society in 1812, is almost sure to be pre-Revolutionary, according to Dr. Harold Jantz of Johns Hopkins University, who has made a close study of the Winthrop collection.[5]

Boston and Philadelphia are the most thoroughly studied areas. Philadelphia information is taken principally from an unpublished thesis written by Charles Hummel at the University of Delaware in 1957 on the influence of English design

2. *William and Mary Quarterly,* series 1, VIII, No. 2, 77-79.
3. *William and Mary Quarterly,* series 1, X, No. 3, 232-241. The inventory of Carter's library appeared in the papers of Philip Vickers Fithian, a member of the class of 1772 at Princeton College, who thereafter was tutor of Carter's children and who died in 1776. Waterman has related details of Nomini Hall to Salmon's *Palladio Londinensis,* probably in the changes which were made ca. 1770, in *Mansions of Virginia* (Chapel Hill, 1946), pp. 143-144.
4. *William and Mary Quarterly,* series 1, VIII, No. 2, 78.
5. From information in a letter from Dr. Jantz, dated 21 April 1960.

books on Philadelphia furniture in the period 1760-1780. Hummel was the first to list systematically the available sources and use them in a study of local decorative influences. Hummel's study produced a list of fifty-one architectural books in Philadelphia during the peak economic period covered by this study.[6] Seven Philadelphia titles have been added in this revision. Titles of architectural books in pre-Revolutionary Boston, including the Harvard College Library, totaled sixty-four, according to the data produced by this survey.

For both Boston and Philadelphia there are booksellers' catalogues, newspaper records, and information on institutional and private collections. The Boston records, including Harvard, provide an accurate picture of the kind and extent of information available. Records exist before 1750, but only five references to architectural books were found in that period (Perrault, in the Samuel Lee catalogue of 1693, Perrault and Wotton at Harvard in 1723, and the two manuals advertised by the bookseller Cox in a catalogue of 1734). The Mather Byles references cannot be dated, although we know that he was ill and inactive during and following the Revolutionary period and that his early books may well have been owned by his grandfather Increase Mather, who died in 1723.[7] Dow's newspaper coverage begins in 1704 with Boston's first newspaper, but the first advertisement for an architectural book is dated 1754. Thereafter, forty-six titles

---

6. Seven titles have been added in this revision.

7. *Dictionary of American Biography*, Charles Scribner's Sons, New York, 1929, v. III, pp. 381-382.

Fig. 3. A door and window in the Tuscan order by Le Muet, in the appendix to Richards' translation of Palladio (courtesy: Avery Library).

9

occur in newspaper and booksellers' catalogue references. The library of Thomas Dawes, a Boston builder born in 1731, also probably was collected around mid-century, since he could not have been active before the 1750's.

A comparable continuity of information exists in Philadelphia, beginning with the records of Franklin's Library Company, founded in 1731. In Newport there are the 1750 and 1764 catalogues of the Redwood Library, and Peter Harrison's important collection of architectural books from the inventory of his estate in 1775. New York is moderately well covered, with five booksellers' catalogues, two catalogues for the New York Society Library, the catalogue of the library belonging to the Corporation of the City of New York in 1766, and the Samuel and William Samuel Johnson libraries at Columbia University. In Charleston there is the 1770 catalogue of the Charleston Library Society, organized in 1748, a 1772 supplement following an important gift, and the source work of Beatrice St. Julien Ravenel.

The most substantial contribution to our knowledge of architectural books in the American colonies before 1750 is the library of William Byrd, who built his house Westover on the James River about 1730 and who died in 1744. A catalogue of his library was made probably about 1751, according to Edwin Wolf II, who compares the library in the colonial period only to those collected by James Logan and Cotton Mather.[8] Byrd owned ten architectural books, a

---

8. Edwin Wolf II, "The Dispersal of the Library of William Byrd of Westover," *Proceedings of the American Antiquarian Society* LXVIII (1959), 19-106.

representative collection all published before 1730, three of them before 1700. Logan at his death in 1751 owned four architectural books, the latest published in 1703. Mather, who died in 1728, mentioned no architectural books in his prideful references to his large library.[9]

In summary, all but four booksellers' references, in newspapers and sales catalogues, and all except five references in institutional collections, occur after 1750. References increase markedly about 1760, as noted also by Hummel, due partly to better information (only four booksellers' catalogues with architectural listings occur before 1760 and all relevant institutional catalogues, except Yale's, were revised after 1760) and partly to increased demand. The libraries of Peter Harrison and William Buckland belong very near the end of the colonial period, although Harrison probably began to collect his architectural books in the 1740's and Buckland certainly by 1755 owned some books. Thomas Dawes actually lived until 1809, but his library represents work dating from mid-century. The William Samuel Johnson books were owned in 1758. The Mather Byles library, inventoried at his death in 1788, may represent more than a hundred years of family book collecting.

The time boundaries of the books in English span a century and a half, from Wotton's *Elements,* first published in 1624, to volume one of Robert and James Adam's *Works in Architecture* of 1773. Twenty-four titles among the

---

9. However, only about 500 of his estimated 3000-4000 books can be identified in this way. Thomas Goddard Wright, *Literary Culture in Early New England, 1620-1730* (New Haven, 1920), pp. 242-253.

references were published before 1715. Of these, six were in Italian, one in French, one appeared in French and in English translation, and the rest were in English. Ten of the English books were published before 1700. Four were English translations from French and two others were selections from Italian sources, Richards' *Palladio* with Le Muet's supplement and William Leybourn's *Scamozzi* with an added description by John James of a method for constructing and using a "joynt rule." Five titles occur between 1700 and 1714, one in French, the rest in English (two translations from French and one from Italian). The next decade, 1715-1725, brought eleven titles which appeared in the American colonies, including major English design books by Campbell and James Leoni.

The most intense publication occurred between 1731 and 1735, when eleven titles were published, five less than the total for the whole decade of the fifties. They were produced by such familiar Palladian authors as James Gibbs, Francis Price, William Salmon, Batty Langley, and Isaac Ware. The preceding five years produced ten titles in the American references, more than in any other five-year period except that of 1731-1735, making a grand total of twenty-one for the decade. These include such American rarities as William Kent's *Designs of Inigo Jones* published in 1727, and the combined production of Kent, Isaac Ware, and Thomas Ripley, *The Designs of Houghton in Norfolk* of 1735, both of which represented the most advanced English design and were apparently owned only by Peter Harrison in the American colonies.

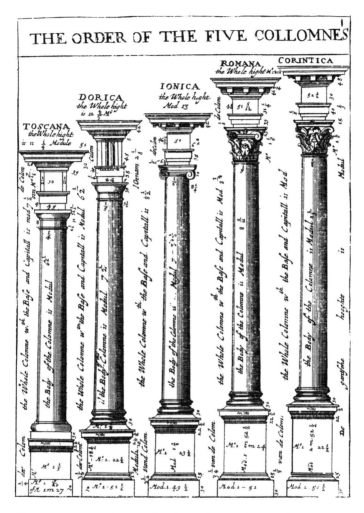

Fig. 4. The orders, from Leyburn's translation of Scamozzi, *The Mirror of Architecture*, 1730 edition (courtesy: Avery Library). First published in 1669.

13

But the proliferation of architectural books depended on the demand for technical knowledge. The intense publication years of 1731-1735 produced the two most frequently used builders' manuals, long on geometry, arithmetic, and structural members, but with no plans and few designs for architectural embellishment. These two manuals, according to the number of references found in this study, appeared in 1733 and 1734, Francis Price's *The British Carpenter* and William Salmon's *Palladio Londinensis.* Price offered extremely basic plates in a handy small folio, showing "the most approved methods of connecting timber together, for most of the various uses in building, with the rules necessary to be observed therein." To these he added plates on the construction of domes and staircases, rules for squaring timbers for "twisted" stair rails, a table for timber scantlings, and general recommendations on strength in construction and spacing of joists. He included a supplement with Palladio's orders, details of entablatures, elliptical and angular pediments, and their "application to use" in doors, windows, and arches. His final contribution was a section on the construction of a trammel, a device for drawing an ellipse which was still in use in the nineteenth century, according to Colvin. He claimed that his plates were so clear that no other information was required, and he was certainly a valuable guide to country workmen trying to follow city fashions.

Salmon's *Palladio Londinensis* was designed to provide the builder with everything he needed to build and decorate a house according to a plan provided in some other source. The third edition was organized in three parts with fifty-two copper plates, and is again a convenient size for the workman on the job. It includes sections on geometric figures, the orders, staircases, chimneypieces, and roofs. Salmon attacked a basic Palladian problem in trying to teach "a young architect" how to determine "a just proportion." He gave directions for finding the module arithmetically, geometrically, and "inspectionally" by a table. He complained about the Italian and French theorists who did not include these vital matters. He thought Halfpenny and Langley the best of his predecessors in this respect, but preferred his own methods because they did away with Langley's troublesome "aliquot" parts besides providing for more variations in use of pilasters and columns. The organization and presentation of the

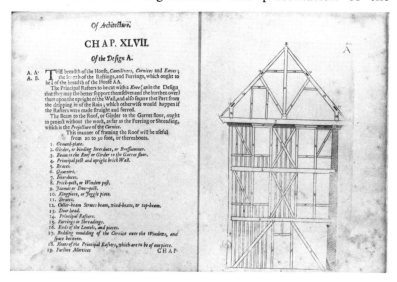

Fig. 5. House framing, Richards' translation of Palladio. This copy belonged to Thomas Dawes (courtesy: Boston Athenaeum).

material in this book throw considerable light on the men who used such manuals. The difficulties involved for a craftsman unskilled in mathematics in achieving a "just proportion" show up in the replacement of fractions with aliquot parts, in turn replaced by a table. Salmon, however, offered methods for those who wanted to work out the problem in order to follow any scheme. Although a more comprehensive volume than Price's, Salmon's is still very basic. Only sixteen plates in the third edition are designs for doors, windows, and chimneypieces. The rest are structural with a section, as in Price, on the construction of various kinds of roofs.

Salmon's book was without doubt aimed at the home market, even the London market, since it includes London's brick fire wall regulations of 1661 for contiguous buildings. It seems unlikely, however, that these extremely useful manuals were produced without the colonial market in mind. There was a consciousness of the need to establish English equality in the artistic sphere now that she was politically and economically dominant, a declared *raison d'être* in Abraham Swan's introduction to his *Collection of Designs* of 1757 and in Batty Langley's exhortation to English craftsmen in his pocket-sized *Golden Rule for Drawing and Working the Five Orders in Architecture* of 1756.

Fig. 6. John Brown's "Joynt-Rule," published in Leyburn's translation of Scamozzi, *The Mirror of Architecture* (courtesy: Avery Library).

16

Langley exploited the receptivity of British craftsmen in a series of books which began to appear in the twenties. They culminated in the influential *The City and Country Builder's and Workmen's Treasury of Designs* of 1740, with the Langleys' *Builder's Jewel* of 1741 the third most often consulted books according to this study. In the *Treasury* Langley incorporated far more designs than his competitors, "upwards of four hundred grand designs . . . on one hundred eighty-six copper plates," which he tended to re-use in his later publications. The *Treasury* is a small-folio collection of designs for important architectural decorative elements (its subtitle is *Or the Art of Drawing and Working the Ornamental Parts of Architecture*), with a supplement of fourteen plates devoted to problems of construction (all of them roofs). There is no section on geometry, but there are directions for proportioning the orders. Langley had, after all, responded to these other requirements earlier and now recognized the usefulness of a collection of designs for embellishing modest houses. In the introduction to the *Treasury*, he explained his purpose, and the function of the workman's handbook:

> As the greatest Part of the Architecture of Andrea Palladio, published by Leoni, Ware, etc. in large Folio's, consists chiefly of Designs of Palaces, Bridges, and Temples, which to workmen are of Little Use, and as those Books are of large Prices, beyond the Reach of many Workmen, and too large for Use at work; I have therefore, for the common Good, extracted from the works of that great Master, all that is useful to Workmen.

The Langleys' *Builder's Jewel: or, The Youth's Instructor and Workman's Remembrancer*, was, they declared, the first pocket companion for the workman with "all the useful Rules and Proportions"—orders, pediments, cupolas, roofs— in twenty-four pages with ninety-nine plates, sixteen of them

17

roofs. The young workman was urged to study in his leisure hours, to "emulate," and "thereby to make himself the most useful both to himself and his country."

William and John Halfpenny exploited the same market over nearly as long a period, and in 1750 began to issue a series of pamphlets covering the new vogue for the Gothic and Chinese. Also, like Robert Morris and Thomas Lightoler, they correctly assessed middle-class requirements and provided plans and brass-tack costs for modest but "elegant" houses, clearly an important service to colonial builders.

By 1755 the market had been glutted with so many popular interpretations of the master Palladio, and so many people had reacted to arbitrary Palladian discipline with Chinese, Gothic, and ancient designs for subsidiary buildings that Robert Sayer, a London printer and bookseller, advertised a treatise with the title:

> Country Five Barr'd Gates, Stiles and Wickets, elegant Pig-styes, beautiful Henhouses, and delightful Cow-cribs, superb Cart-houses, magnificent Barn Doors, variegated Barn Racks, and admirable Sheep-Folds; according to the Turkish and Persian manner; . . . To which is added, some Designs of Fly-Traps, Bee Palaces, and Emmet Houses, in the Muscovite and Arabian Architecture; all adapted to the Latitude and Genius of England. The whole entirely new, and inimitably designed in Two Parts, on Forty Pewter Plates, under the immediate Inspection of Don Gulielmus De Demi Je ne Sçai Quoi, chief Achitect to the Grand Signior.[10]

Of the sixty-seven titles sold by booksellers (fifty-seven percent of the total American references), the earliest references are to seventeenth century manuals in Boston and one of undetermined date advertised by Benjamin Franklin in

---

10. Noted by H. M. Colvin in *A Biographical Dictionary of English Architects, 1660-1840* (London, 1954), p. 394.

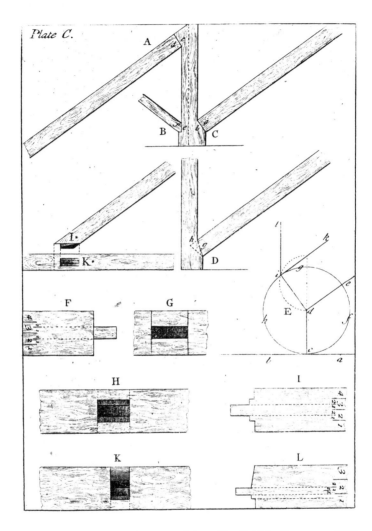

Fig. 7. Framing timbers, from Price, *The British Carpenter*, 1753 (courtesy: Avery Library).

Philadelphia in 1744. The next references are to books published during the saturated five-year period of 1731-1735, to Salmon's *Palladio Londinensis* in 1751, and to Price's *British Carpenter* in 1754 in Philadelphia, although the *British Carpenter* was in the Library Company in 1739, a significant comment on its usefulness. The next Boston reference is in 1754, to Leybourn's translation of Scamozzi, one of four seventeenth century books to appear in the booksellers' references. Leybourn's inclusion of John Brown's *Description and Use of a Joynt Rule* is comparable to Price's directions for constructing a trammel and must have made Leybourn's one of the most important of the early English publications. The Price and Salmon manuals, apparently the most often used in the American colonies, do not occur in Boston advertisements until 1761, a significant delay.

An abrupt rise in demand is discernible for the books published after 1730. Of the eleven books which appear in the crowded 1731-1735 period, eight occur among the booksellers' references. Six were available in Philadelphia, five in Boston and three in New York. The fact that New York's expansion came two decades later than Philadelphia's must account to some extent for the scarcity of references in New York generally (a total of twenty-six for the booksellers, and thirty altogether). It may be that the pattern established by George Mason and William Buckland at Gunston Hall is characteristic of river plantation building,[11] and that the Van Rensselaers and Livingstones hired architects with their own

---

11. See Rosamond R. Beirne and John H. Scarff, *William Buckland, 1733-1774* (Baltimore, 1958).

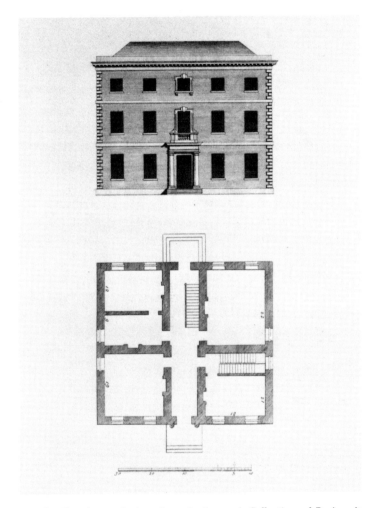

Fig. 8. Elevation and plan, from A. Swan, *A Collection of Designs in Architecture*, 1757 (courtesy: Avery Library).

21

libraries of handbooks for which few records remain. Three architects advertised in the *New York Mercury* in the years 1758, 1765, and 1768, while three house carpenters in the years 1768-1771 advertised that they would undertake designs for buildings.[12] Architects advertised in Philadelphia, too, and in Annapolis and Charleston.[13] Furthermore, it is interesting to note that in Williamsburg, where there is little specific information on handbooks, an architect advertised in the *Virginia Gazette* in 1777 that he had "an elegant Assortment of Tools, and Books of Architect, which I imported from London and Liverpool."[14]

The significant difference in availability, however, is between Philadelphia and Boston, where information is good. Forty-eight books were advertised for sale in Boston, and forty-three in Philadelphia. Twenty of the books advertised in Philadelphia were apparently not available in Boston. Eleven of those were published in the fifties, the decade of attempts to enliven the severity of Burlington-Campbell Palladianism. Two of the twenty must have been in Boston (Gibbs' *Rules for Drawing the Several Parts of Architecture*, 1732, and Swan's *Designs in Carpentry*, 1759), although apparently not advertised, because they appear in the Dawes library, in general an extremely conservative collection in

---

12. *The Arts and Crafts in New York, 1726-1776, Advertisements and News Items from New York City Newspapers* (New York, 1938).

13. *The Arts and Crafts in Philadelphia, Maryland and South Carolina, 1721-1785*, gleanings from newspapers collected by Alfred Coxe Prime (The Walpole Society, 1929).

14. Lester J. Cappon and Stella F. Duff, *Virginia Gazette Index, 1736-1780* (Williamsburg, 1950), and accompanying microfilm.

Fig. 9. Designs for fireplaces, from A. Swan, *The British Architect*, the third edition of 1758 (courtesy: Avery Library). The first edition date of 1745 has been removed from the plates.

23

which more than half of the books were originally published before mid-century. While twenty-five of the books advertised in Boston were unavailable in Philadelphia, only nine were published in the fifties. They included Abraham Swan's important *Collection of Designs*, 1757, but not the Halfpenny pamphlets in the new styles. Langley, on the other hand, remained a constant in both Philadelphia and Boston, and he and Hoppus revised their earlier handbooks to include new motifs. Boston had access to fashionable designs also in Morris's *Architecture Improved* and Swan's *British Architect* of the preceding decade, but used them sparingly. Although the Chinese influence was present in Crunden's *Chinese Railings and Gates*, conservative Boston apparently clung to fundamental classicism in architectural sources. Henry Knox in the years just preceding the break with England was selling volume one of Adam's *Designs in Architecture*, Chambers' *Civil Architecture*, and Riou's *Grecian Orders*, setting the stage for federal classicism and leaving the ornate richness of the rococo to the opulent South.

Demand was maintained for virtually all the books published from the 1731 surge. All books published in the forties which appear in the American references were available from booksellers. In the fifties, only Halfpenny's *Designs for Chinese Temples* fails to occur among these references. The failure to find a reference to the Halfpenny pamphlet probably represents a flaw in the survey system. The earlier monumental folio publications were not popular, but they were influential. Campbell, Leoni, and Kent were not advertised but were found usually in a progressive institutional

24

Fig. 10. A staircase, from A. Swan, *The British Architect*, the third edition of 1758 (courtesy: Avery Library).

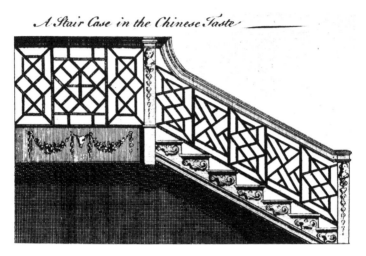

Fig. 11. A staircase, from Halfpenny, *New Designs for Chinese Temples*, 1750 (courtesy: Avery Library).

library like that of the Library Company of Philadelphia, or in the private collections of a gentleman scholar like Byrd or an architect like Harrison.

By 1760, the gap between publication date and arrival in the colonies was closing. Ten of the twelve books published in the fifties and available in Philadelphia were there in 1760. In two instances Boston was only a year behind, and William Pain's *Builder's Companion,* published in 1758, appears in both Philadelphia and Boston advertisements in 1760. The Pain instance is especially significant, since the book had considerable influence in New England in the early post-Revolutionary years. Again, in this late period, two out of three of John Crunden's handbooks were available in Boston and not in Philadelphia, which suggests the importance of Crunden too in Boston in the period preceding the Adamesque.

But exploitation of the rococo was definitely left to the new merchant aristocracy to the south. Its enthusiastic reception in the sixties in Philadelphia and Maryland coincides with economic expansion which made Philadelphia the third city in the Empire at the outbreak of the Revolution.

William Buckland, architect of Gunston Hall, worked in Annapolis from 1770 to 1774, at the height of the demand for internal embellishment. He owned thirteen architectural books.[15] Among them were Swan's *British Architect* of 1745, which brought the rococo to the colonies, his *Collection of Designs in Architecture* and the *Designs in Carpentry*, both published in the fifties, Lightoler's *Gentleman and Farmer's Architect*, which supplemented Swan's big *Collection of Designs* with more plans for modest houses (Swan notes that he intended Book II to be a collection of designs for more elaborate houses, but he changed his mind because designs for smaller houses were more useful), and Langley's *Gothic Architecture.*

---

15. These are listed in the inventory of Buckland's estate in the Maryland archives, and were published by Beirne and Scarff in *William Buckland.* Buckland also owned Thomas Chippendale, *The Gentleman and Cabinet-Maker's Director*, which included eight plates on proportioning the orders as a necessary architectural background to cabinet-making. The first edition of 1754 also included three plates demonstrating perspective drawing of chairs, a dressing table and a bookcase. The perspective plates were dropped by 1762 when the enlarged third edition appeared with two hundred plates compared to one hundred and sixty in the first edition. Chippendale was advertised in Boston by Cox and Berry probably in 1772 (see *Sources*).

The combination of merchant prince and architect occurred in New England. The influence of Peter Harrison of Newport must have been enormous. He owned a large and representative collection of twenty-seven architectural books ranging in date from 1664 to 1766, from John Evelyn's translation of Frêart de Chambray's *Parallel of the Ancient Architecture with the Modern* to Overton's *Original Designs of Temples and Other Ornamental Buildings.* He seems to have collected his architectural library systematically from the whole period of English publication and some of the most important books were apparently unique in the American colonies. He bought nine in the dense publication decade of 1726-1735, and seven more volumes were added during the flurry of the fifties. He acquired only four of those published in the forties, but significantly these included Swan's *British Architect,* which introduced the Rococo to the colonies and Halfpenny's *New and Complete System of Architecture,* which provided plans specifically for small "elegant" houses admirably suited to the colonial market. To compare the Harrison collection with that of the only other New England architect or builder whom we know, one third of Harrison's collection dates from 1750, as do four of the eleven identifiable books owned by Thomas Dawes. [16] Dawes' collection was generally very conservative. He did not

16. Twelve titles are listed from the Dawes estate in the 1809 acquisition book of the Boston Athenaeum. The twelfth, listed as "Jones' Designs," can no longer be traced in the Athenaeum collection. It conceivably was Kent's *Designs of Inigo Jones.* If it were, it would be a significant addition to the Boston list.

own the significant innovating books of the forties, and while two of his later books were lesser Swan publications, the others were Riou's *Architecture of Stone Bridges* and Pain's conservative *Builder's Companion.* Two of Dawes' very basic books, however, were in late editions, Hoppus's *Repository* in the 1760 edition and Langley's *Treasury* in the third edition of 1756. This means of course that even without the volumes bringing the Rococo and Chinese, he had some choice of decorative detail in the new modes since Langley and Hoppus quickly adapted their old standards to the new taste. However, he never owned any of the major new books of design.

To an important degree, Harrison's architectural library must represent all the main elements in the English movement after the Restoration. His earliest books are French, Fréart's *Parallel of the Ancient Architecture with the Modern* and LeClerc's *Treatise of Architecture,* which Byrd also owned. Although Holland was the earliest channel taken by the Italian Renaissance in reaching England, by 1660 the hiatus in building caused by the Puritan revolution, political and economic difficulties with the Netherlands, and the cultural and political dominance of France in seventeenth-century Europe naturally led to French references in beginning Palladianism in colonial America. Nothing in the American records antedates the Restoration except Harvard's Italian theory, all added after the library fire of 1764, Wotton's *Elements* at Harvard in 1723, and the 1649 edition of Vitruvius published in Amsterdam, owned by James Logan and the Charleston Library Society, the only direct link to

29

the Netherlands. The earliest references at Harvard, to Perrault listed with Wotton's *Elements* in 1723, are French and
English. The aristocratic confidence of the French Academy
in its ability to codify the production of art inevitably gave
strength to the essentially middle-class, rational application
of geometric formulae to popular building in England and her
colonies.

# SOURCES

Professor John Coolidge, Director of the Fogg Museum at Harvard, has been the source of countless valuable suggestions, and indeed suggested this study.

Titles and edition dates of English architectural books have been checked in H. M. Colvin, *A Biographical Dictionary of English Architects, 1660-1840* (London, 1954). Early English titles have been checked in the catalogue of the British Museum. French and Italian books have been checked in the *Catalog of the Royal Institute of British Architects* (1937). Edition dates for Italian books are those of the actual volumes as recorded, plus first edition dates when they were readily available. Additional edition data have been taken from the Elizabeth Baer catalogue of the Fowler Collection of Architectural Books at Johns Hopkins (Evergreen House Foundation, Baltimore, 1961) for numbers 2, 13, 48, 51, 76, 83, and 85 in this list. Moxon, Neve, and Ralph were also checked in the R.I.B.A. catalogue. For most of the books listed, one or more editions have been examined in the Avery Library, the Huntington Library in San Marino, California, or the Library Company of Philadelphia.

In all other instances, edition dates derive from the helpful response of librarians in the institutions listed under "Modern Locations." The detailed bibliographical data supplied by the Boston Athenaeum, Colonial Williamsburg, the Library Company of Philadelphia, and Winterthur, in particular, have filled many gaps.

## BOSTON

*A Catalogue of Books in all Arts and Sciences; To be Sold at the Shop of T. Cox, Bookseller*, at the Lamb, on the South Side of the Town-House in Boston, June 30, 1734. American Antiquarian Society. In Readex Microprint edition of *Early American Imprints*, published by the American Antiquarian Society, based on Charles Evans' *American Bibliography*, 1903-1934, privately printed for the author by the Columbia Press, Chicago, vols. 13-14 by Clifford K. Shipton, 1955 and 1959, published by the American Antiquarian Society, Worcester, Mass., *Supplement* by Roger P. Bristol, University Press of Virginia, Charlottesville, 1970.

*A Catalogue of Mein's Circulating Library Consisting of about Twelve Hundred Volumes, in most Branches of Polite*

*Literature, Arts and Sciences* (Boston), facsim. from MHS Photostat Americana, 2nd series, 1936, in the Boston Public Library, 1765.

Another Mein *Catalogue* [1766?]. American Antiquarian Society. (The date attributed to the catalogue in this, as in other instances where exact dates are missing, is that attributed by the institution involved.)

*A Catalogue of New and Old Books Which Will be Exhibited by Auction, by Robert Bell, Bookseller and Auctioneer on July 4, 1770* ... at Royal Exchange Tavern, King Street, Boston. Photostat of a broadside in the Bowdoin Papers, vol. xii, MHS.

*A Catalogue of Books* ... Cox and Berry, King Street, Boston [1772?]. American Antiquarian Society.

*A Catalogue of Books Imported & to be Sold by Henry Knox*, at the London Book-Store, a little Southward of the Towne-House, in Cornhill (Boston, 1773). Boston Public Library.

The Knox Papers in the Massachusetts Historical Society.

Dowe, George Francis, *The Arts and Crafts in New England, 1704-1775* (Topsfield, Mass.: The Wayside Press, 1927).

Library of Thomas Dawes, from a list of his books in the Boston Athenaeum Accession Book, 1809, when the books were given to the Athenaeum. Most of these have been located and identified in the Athenaeum collection by Dr. Abbott Lowell Cummings, Director of the Society for the Preservation of New England Antiquities.

Mather Byles, manuscript catalogue of his library at his death in 1788, in the Massachusetts Historical Society. Reproduced and brought to my attention by Edwin Wolf II, Librarian of the Library Company of Philadelphia.

## CHARLESTON

Charleston Library Society, *A Catalogue of Books, 1770*, from a list of relevant volumes supplied by the assistant librarian, Mrs. W. H. Haigh. The catalogue is also in the Library of Congress and is reproduced in the Readex Microprint edition of *Early American Imprints, op cit.*

Supplement to the Charleston Library Society *Catalogue of Books*, 1772, in the Library of Congress.

*Architects of Charleston*, Beatrice St. Julien Ravenel, Carolina Art Association, Charleston, 1945.

*The Arts and Crafts in Philadephia, Maryland and South Carolina, 1721-1785*, gleanings from newspapers collected by Alfred Coxe Prime (The Walpole Society, 1929).

## NEW HAVEN

*A Catalogue of Books*, sold by Benedict Arnold [1765?]. Toledo Museum broadside, Readex Microprint, *op. cit.*

## NEWPORT

Bridenbaugh, Carl, *Peter Harrison, First American Architect* (Chapel Hill, University of North Carolina Press, 1949).

Peter Harrison inventory, in Connecticut State Archives, Hartford.

REDWOOD LIBRARY:

Catalogue of 1750 (relevant volumes extracted by the librarian, Donald T. Gibbs).

Catalogue of 1764, published in Fiske Kimball, *Thomas Jefferson, Architect* (Boston, 1916), p. 34n.

## NEW YORK

*A Catalogue of Books* . . . to be Sold by Garrat Noel, Bookseller in Dock-Street, New York, 1754. American Antiquarian Society.

*A Catalogue of Books in History, Divinity, Law, Arts and Sciences, and the Several Parts of Polite Literature;* to be Sold by Garrat Noel, Bookseller in Dock-Street (New York, 1755), Boston Public Library.

*A Catalogue of Books* . . . (New York, 1773). Houghton Library, Harvard University.

Hummel, Charles, *Influence of English Design Books on Philadelphia Cabinet Makers, 1760-1780*, Part II, Section 2 (University of Delaware Master's Thesis, 1952), which includes a study of two New York booksellers' catalogues: James Rivington, *A Catalogue of Books, Lately Imported and Sold by James Rivington* . . ., also at His Store next door to Messrs. Taylor and Cox, in Front-Street, Philadelphia (New York, 1760); and James Rivington, and Brown, *A Catalogue of Books, Sold by Rivington and Brown* . . . (New York, 1762).

New York Society Library, *A Catalogue of the Books Belonging to the New York Society Library* (1754). Photostat of original in the New York Society Library.

35

*A Catalogue of the Library Belonging to the City of New York*, 1766. Henry E. Huntington Library. In Readex Microprint series, *op. cit.*

*The Arts and Crafts in New York 1726-1776, Advertisements and News Items from New York City Newspapers* (New York). Printed for the *New York Historical Society*, 1938.

*Libraries of William and William Samuel Johnson, first and third presidents of King's College (Columbia University)* in the Butler Library of Columbia University.

PHILADELPHIA

Hummel, *op. cit.* Includes information from the minute books of the Library Company, letter books and broadsides for Philadelphia booksellers David Hall and William Strahan, as well as Rivington and Brown, files of the *Pennsylvania Gazette*, the *Pennsylvania Journal and Weekly Advertiser*, and the *New York Mercury*.

Edwin Wolf II, librarian of the Library Company, looked at the Philadelphia references in detail, corrected and clarified many points, and in several instances was able to move a date of record back by a number of years.

*Catalog of the Library Company* (1741), facsim. published by the LCP in 1956.

*Catalog of the Library Company* (1770), in Kimball, *Jefferson*, pp. 34-35n.

*The Arts and Crafts in Philadelphia, Maryland and South Carolina, 1721-1785*, gleanings from newspapers collected by Alfred Coxe Prime (The Walpole Society, 1929).

*A Catalogue of Books*, sold by B. Franklin, 1744. University of Pennsylvania. In Readex Microprint series, *op. cit.*

*A Catalogue of Books to be Sold by William Bradford* [1764?]. New York Public Library. In Readex Microprint series, *op. cit.*

*A Catalogue of Books to be Sold by John Sparhawk at the London Bookstore* [1773?]. Brown University. In Readex Microprint series, *op. cit.*

## UNIVERSITIES

HARVARD COLLEGE:

*Catalogus Librorum Bibliothecae Collegii Harvardini ...*, compiled by Joshua Lee (Boston, 1723). Houghton Library, Harvard.

A Supplement ... (1725). Houghton Library, Harvard.

A Supplement ... (1735). Houghton Library, Harvard.

*An Alphabetical List of the Books Belonging to the Library of Harvard College*, compiled by Andrew Eliot MS (1765), in the Harvard Archives.

*An Alphabetical List of the Books Belonging to the Library of Harvard College*, compiled by Amos Adams MS (1771), Harvard Archives.

YALE COLLEGE:

*A Catalogue of the Library of Yale College in New Haven* (New London, 1743). Facsim. published by Yale to commemorate opening of Sterling Library.

OTHER

Library of William Buckland (died Baltimore, 1774): Copy of Buckland inventory made by Mr. John Parker, librarian at the Peabody Institute, Baltimore. See also R. R. Beirne and J. H. Scarff, *William Buckland 1733-1774* (Baltimore, 1958).

Library of Mather Byles: See Boston.

Library of William Byrd II: *The Writings of Colonel William Byrd of Westover in Virginia, Esqr.,* John Spencer Bassett (ed.) (New York, 1901), Appendix A; Edwin Wolf II, "The Dispersal of the Library of William Byrd of Westover," *Proceedings of the American Antiquarian Society* LXVIII (1959), 19-106.

Library of Thomas Dawes: 1809 Accession Book, Boston Athenaeum.

Library of Peter Harrison: See Newport.

Libraries of William and William Samuel Johnson: See New York.

Library of James Logan: Included in Hummel's study of Philadelphia. Mr. Edwin Wolf II adds that although the Loganian Catalogue was published in 1760, it represented the books in Logan's library at his death in 1751, and that about 1765 books belonging to his brother, Dr. William Logan of Bristol, England, were sent to Philadelphia and added to the Loganian Library. Two of William Logan's books were architectural and they are designated LL65 in the bibliography.

# Number of References to the Listed Books

| | | Ref. | Year of Pub. | *Earliest Recorded American Reference* |
|---|---|---|---|---|
| 1. | Salmon, *Palladio Londinensis* | 31 | 1734 | 1751 |
| 2. | Price, *British Carpenter* | 27 | 1733 | 1739 |
| 3. | Langley, *Builder's Jewel* | 23 | 1746 | 1755 |
| | Langley, *Builder's Treasury* | 23 | 1740 | 1754 |
| 4. | Swan, *British Architect* | 22 | 1745 | 1760 |
| 5. | Hoppus, *Builder's Repository* | 19 | 1738 | 1751 |
| 6. | Halfpenny, *New and Complete System* | 16 | 1749 | 1755 |
| 7. | Gibbs, *Architecture* | 13 | 1728 | 1760 |
| | Swan, *Collection of Designs* | 13 | 1757 | 1762 |
| 8. | Ware, *Palladio* | 12 | 1737 | 1754 |
| 9. | Pain, *Builder's Companion* | 11 | 1758 | 1760 |
| 10. | Langley, *Builder's Assistant* | 10 | ? (4th ed. 1766) | 1755 |
| 11. | Langley, *Workman's Golden Rule* | 9 | 1756 | 1760 |
| 12. | Hawney, *Measurer* | 8 | 1717 | 1734 |
| | Salmon, *London and Country Builder* | 8 | 1745 | 1755 |
| | Ware, *Complete Body of Architecture* | 8 | 1756 | 1760 |
| 13. | Halfpenny, *Builder's Pocket Companion* | 6 | 1728 | 1761 |
| | Jores, *New Book of Iron Work* | 6 | 1759 | 1762 |
| | Swan, *Designs in Carpentry* | 6 | 1759 | 1773 |
| 14. | Gibbs, *Rules for Drawing* | 5 | 1732 | 1754 |
| | Halfpenny, *Modern Builder's Assistant* | 5 | 1742 | 1760 |
| | Halfpenny, *Useful Architecture* | 5 | 1752 | 1757 |

39

|  | Ref. | Year of Pub. | Earliest Recorded American Reference |
|---|---|---|---|
| Langley, *Builder's Chest Book* | 5 | 1727 | 1760 |
| Langley, *Builder's Director* | 5 | 1746 | 1765 |
| 15. *Builder's Dictionary* | 4 | 1734 | 1750 |
| Campbell, *Vitruvius Britannicus* | 4 | 1715-25 | 1741 |
| Garrett, *Designs . . . for Farm Houses* | 4 | 1747 | 1762 |
| Leoni, *Palladio* | 4 | 1715-16 | 1732 |
| Morris, *Architecture Improved* | 4 | 1755 | 1760 |
| Neve, *Dictionary* | 4 | 1703 | 1743 |
| Perrault, *On the Five Orders* | 4 | 1708 (Paris 1683) | 1723 |
| Riou, *Short Principles* | 4 | 1760 | 1773 |
| Salmon, *Builder's Guide* | 4 | 1736 | 1754 |
| Salmon, *Country Builder's Estimator* | 4 | 1736 | 1760 |
| Wotton, *Elements* | 4 | 1624 | 1723 |
| 16. Adam, *Works in Architecture* | 3 | 1773 | 1773 |
| Chambers' *Treatise* | 3 | 1759 | 1765 |
| Fréart, Sieur de Chambray, *Parallel* | 3 | 1664 | 1770 |
| Halfpenny, *Perspective* | 3 | 1731 | 1761 |
| Halfpenny, *Twelve Beautiful Designs* | 3 | 1749 | 1760 |
| Hoppus, *Practical Measuring* | 3 | 1761 | 1765 |
| Langley, *Ancient Masonry* | 3 | 1736 | 1765 |
| LeClerc, *Traité* | 3 | 1714 | 1761 |
| Morris, *Select Architecture* | 3 | 1757 | 1760 |
| Richards, *Palladio* | 3 | 1663 | 1744 |
| Riou, *Grecian Orders* | 3 | 1768 | 1773 |
| Swan, *Upwards of 150 New Designs* | 3 | 1765 | 1772 |
| Ware, *Designs of Inigo Jones* | 3 | 1735 | 1754 |

40

| | *Ref.* | *Year of Pub.* | *Earliest Recorded American Reference* |
|---|---|---|---|
| 17. Halfpenny, *Art of Sound Building* | 2 | 1725 | 1775 |
| Halfpenny, *Practical Architecture* | 2 | 1724 | 1772 |
| Halfpenny, *Rural Architecture* | 2 | 1752 | 1760 |
| Leoni, *Alberti* | 2 | 1726 | ca.1751 |
| Leyburn, *Scamozzi* | 2 | 1669 | ca. 1751 |
| Morris, *Lectures* | 2 | 1734-36 | 1773 |
| Moxon, *Practical Perspective* | 2 | 1670 | ca. 1751 |
| Vitruvius, *De Architettura* | 2 | 1483 | 1751 |

### SINGLE REFERENCES

| | | |
|---|---|---|
| Barker, *Measurer's Guide* | 1692 | c. 1700 |
| Barozzio, *Regola* | 1563 | 1765 |
| Baretti, *New Book* | 1766 | 1767 |
| Castell, *Villas of the Ancients* | 1728 | 1757 |
| Copland, *New Book* | 1746 | 1775 |
| Crunden, *Carpenter's Companion* | 1765 | 1767 |
| Crunden, *Convenient and Ornamental Architecture* | 1767 | 1773 |
| Crunden, *Joyner's and Cabinet-Maker's Darling* | 1765 | 1767 |
| Darling, *Carpenter's Rule* | 1658 | ? (MB) |
| Decker, *Chinese Architecture* | 1759 | 1760 |
| Dubreuil, *Practice of Perspective* | 1726 | 1741 |
| Ferrerio, *Palazzi* | 1655 | 1744 |
| Fletcher, *Universal Measurer* | 1752-53 | 1773 |
| Foster, *Art of Measuring* | 1652 | ? (MB) |
| Fournier, *Perspective* | 1761 | 1773 |
| Halfpenny, *Country Gentleman's Pocket Companion* | 1753 | 1760 |

| | Year of Pub. | Earliest Recorded American Reference |
|---|---|---|
| Halfpenny, *Chinese Temples* | 1750-55 | 1775 |
| Halfpenny, *Chinese Lattices* | ? (2nd ed. 1755) | 1760 |
| Johnson, *150 New Designs* | 1761 | 1774 |
| Keay, *Practical Measurer* | 1718 | 1762 |
| Kent, *Inigo Jones* | 1727 | 1775 |
| Labelye, *Westminster Bridge* | 1751 | 1773 |
| Langley, *Carpenter's Companion* | ? | 1776 |
| Langley, *Gothic* | 1742 | 1774 |
| Langley, *London Prices* | 1748 | 1772 |
| Langley, *Prac. Geometry* | 1726 | 1746 |
| LeClerc, *Geometry* | 1727 (3rd ed.) | 1770 |
| Lightoler, *Gentleman's and Farmer's Architect* | 1762 | 1774 |
| Mandey, *Measuring* | 1682 | 1734 |
| Miles, *Practical Measurer* | 1740 (2nd ed.) | 1772 |
| Miller, *Elements of Architecture* | ca. 1748 | 1763 |
| Morris, *Essay in Defense of Ancient Architecture* | 1728 | 1775 |
| Moxon, *Theory and Practice of Architecture* | 1728 | 1775 |
| Noble, *Perspective* | 1771 | 1772 |
| Oakley, *Complete Builder* | 1738 | 1767 |
| Oakley, *Magazine* | 1730 | 1750 |
| Over, *Ornamental Architecture* | 1758 | 1760 |
| Overton, *Original Designs* | 1766 | 1775 |
| Pain, *Builder's Pocket Treasure* | 1763 | 1773 |
| Palladio, *L'architettura* | 1570 | 1765 |

| | *Year of Pub.* | *Earliest Recorded American Reference* |
|---|---|---|
| Partridge, *Double Scale* | 1671 | 1734 |
| Pozzo, *Perspective* | 1707 | 1750 |
| Ralph, *Critical Review* | 1734 | 1764 |
| Rusconi, *Del l'architettura* | 1590 | 1765 |
| Serlio, *Tutte L'opere* | 1584 | 1765 |
| Smith, *Carpenter's Companion* | 1733 | 1764 |
| *Several Prospects of . . . Buildings in London* | 1724 | 1770 |
| Sturmy, *Architecture, etc.* | ? | 1744 |
| Taylor, *Perspective* | 1715 (Kirby, 1754) | 1773 |
| Ware, Kent, Ripley, *Designs of Houghton* | 1735 | 1775 |

# Eighteenth-Century Location Symbols

Numbers following these symbols indicate the earliest date of record for each book in the locality represented by the symbol. Since all dates but one fall within the eighteenth century, the first two digits, except in that case, have been omitted. Dates are not used with symbols representing individuals because in each case information is based on an inventory taken in a specified year. Both the Association Library and the Union Library Company merged with the Library Company of Philadelphia before 1770. Parentheses around an LCP notation in the body of the list indicate that in all probability the volume in question came from one of these other institutions.

43

Numbers in parentheses below represent the number of books available in each locality during the whole period under consideration. Numbers in the second line of each listing are the numbers of the books in each locality as they occur in this list.

ALCP Association Library Company of Philadelphia (2)
58, 80

B William Byrd II, died 1744, library catalogued ca. 1751 (10)
5, 14, 19, 46, 47, 48, 49, 56, 69, (?)

Bb Boston booksellers (48)
1, 3, 7, 9, 11, 16, 17, 20, 23, 25, 28, 31, 32, 34, 35, 38, 39, 40, 41, 42, 45, 46, 49, 52, 53, 59, 63, 64, 67, 70, 72, 73, 74, 75, 79, 80, 82, 84, 86, 106, 107, 108, 109, 111, 112, 113, 114, 116

Bu William Buckland, inventory at death, 1774 (13)
17, 31, 32, 33, 42, 43, 50, 52, 75, 79, 80, 81, 84

MB Mather Byles, inventory at death, 1788 (5)
13, 26, 35, 102, 104

CCM Carpenter's Company of Philadelphia Member (3)
63, 67, 79

CLS Charleston Library Society (11)
4, 7, 13, 15, 17, 18, 63, 75, 86, 110, 119

TD Thomas Dawes, died 1809, library given to Boston Athenaeum, 1809 (12)
5, 17, 18, 31, 42, 63, 69, 70, 75, 81, 82, (?)

PH  Peter Harrison, inventory at death, 1775 (27)
    8, 15, 17, 18, 19, 22, 23, 24, 26, 27, 34, 36, 42, 46,
    52, 53, 54, 55, 62, 63, 75, 79, 80, 81, 84, 85, 87

HCL  Harvard College Library (10 titles, 11 books)
     2, 7, 47, 65, 66, 71, 76, 83, 106, 119

WSJ  William Samuel Johnson, books owned in 1758 (2)
     74, 106

LCP  Library Company of Philadelphia (21)
     1, 4, 5, 6, 13, 17, 18, 30, 37, 44, 47, 48, 58, 66, 67,
     75, 77, 79, 80, 84, 86

LL  Loganian Library, 1751 and 1765 (6)
    57, 58, 66, 69, 83, 119

NHb  New Haven bookseller (1)
     75

NYb  New York booksellers (26)
     12, 16, 17, 21, 22, 27, 28, 29, 30, 34, 38, 41, 42,
     45, 52, 55, 61, 63, 67, 72, 73, 74, 75, 79, 84, 86

NYCC  New York City Corporation Library (1)
      15

NYSL  New York Society Library (3)
      5, 30, 31

Pb  Philadelphia booksellers (43)
    4, 10, 12, 16, 17, 18, 20, 21, 22, 23, 26, 27, 28, 29,
    30, 31, 34, 37, 38, 39, 41, 42, 45, 51, 52, 55, 61,
    63, 67, 72, 73, 74, 75, 79, 80, 81, 84, 85, 103, 105,
    106, 117, 118

PCC Philadelphia, Christ Church Library (1)
101

RL Redwood Library (7)
4, 60, 67, 68, 75, 78, 86

ULCP Union Library Company of Philadelphia (7)
37, 48, 58, 66, 67, 80, 86

JW Joseph Wragg, estate inventory at death, c.
1751-1753 (6)
5, 15, 19, 66, 74, 115

Y Yale (2)
47, 58

# Modern Location Symbols

A Avery Library, Columbia University

BaP Baltimore, George Peabody Department of Enoch
Pratt Free Library

BA Boston Athenaeum

BPL Boston Public Library

Br Brown University

CLS Charleston Library Society

CW Colonial Williamsburg

C Cornell

D Dartmouth

F Fowler Collection, Johns Hopkins

HCL  Harvard University

HH  Henry E. Huntington Library

JCB  John Carter Brown Library, Brown University

JH  Johns Hopkins

LC  Library of Congress

LCP  Library Company of Philadelphia

NcC  University of North Carolina, Chapel Hill

NcD  North Carolina, Duke University

NcG  University of North Carolina, Greensboro

NcRS  University of North Carolina, Raleigh

NYM  New York, Metropolitan Museum

NYP  New York Public Library

NYSL  New York Society Library

O  Ohio State University

PF  Free Library of Philadelphia

PrA  Providence Athenaeum[1]

PrP  Providence Public Library

RL  Redwood Library

RI  Rhode Island School of Design

---

1. The 1768 catalogue of the Providence Library, now Athenaeum, includes Salmon's *Palladio Londinensis* (1748) and Langley's *Builder's Compleat Assistant* (1738). Joseph Brown (1736-1803) of Providence owned Gibbs' *Architecture* from which he took the design of the First Baptist Meeting House of 1775 in Providence. This information is from unpublished work done in 1958 by Dr. H. F. Koeper, Professor of Architecture, California Polytechnic University, Pomona.

SPNEA Society for the Preservation of New England
Antiquities

UCB University of California, Berkeley

UCLA University of California, Los Angeles

UP University of Pennsylvania

USC University of Southern California

UV University of Virginia

VHS Virginia Historical Society

W Winterthur

Y Yale

# A LIST OF
# ARCHITECTURAL BOOKS
# AVAILABLE IN AMERICA
# BEFORE
# THE REVOLUTION

The numbers to the right of the listings indicate time divisions for the whole period of publication represented:

1—before 1700
2—1700-1725
3—1726-1744
4—1745-1759
5—1760-1775

1. Adam, Robert and James, *Works in Architecture,*   5
   Vol. 1, 1773 (vols. 2 and 3, 1822, posthumously).
   Bb74, LCP74[1]
   A, BA, BaP, CW, C, HCL, HH, JCB, LCP, NYM,
   NYP, NYSL, NcD, O, PrP, UCB, UV, W, Y

2. Barozzio, Giacomo (da Vignola), *Regola delli*   1
   *Cinque Ordini D'Architettura,* Rome, 1563.
   HCL65
   BA, CW, F, HCL, HH, JH, NcD, NYM, NYP, PF,
   RL, VHS, W

3. Baretti, –, *New Book of Ornaments for the Year*   5
   *1766, Very Useful for Cabinetmakers, Carvers,*
   *Painters, Engravers, Chasers, etc.*[2]
   Bb67

4. *The Builder's Dictionary, or Gentleman and Archi-*   3
   *tect's Companion,* 2 vols., London, 1734.
   RL50, Pb54, LCP57, CLS72
   A, BA, CW, C, HH, JCB, LC, LCP, NcD, NYP,
   NYSL, RL, UP, UV, VHS, W

---

1. Mr. Wolf has informed me that Library Company of Philadelphia records show that while volume 1 was ordered in 1773, it was not present in the Library until 1774. Two bills in the Knox papers in the Massachusetts Historical Society, one undated and one dated July 29, 1774, show two copies of two volumes of, in one case, "Adam's Designs" and in the other "Adam's Architecture."

2. This is the only reference found for this book. It was advertised by Henry Webley, Crunden's publisher, in a circular dated 20 November 1765, bound with Crunden's *Joyner and Cabinet-Maker's Darling* in the Huntington Library's copy. This listing and no. 8 are perhaps not strictly architectural books, and they represent the sort of arbitrary decisions on inclusion which are necessary in preparing a list of this kind. They were included as probable sources for Rococo detail.

5. Campbell, Colen, *Vitruvius Britannicus*, 3 vols.,  2
London, 1715 (vol. 2, 1717; vol. 3, 1725; vols. 4
and 5, 1767 and 1771, by Woolfe and Gandon,
Architects).[3]
LCP41, NYSL58, B, TD, JW
A, BaP, BA, CLS, CW, C, F, HCL, HH, JCB, JH,
LC, LCP, NcD, NcRS, NYM, NYP, NYSL, O, PF,
RL, SPNEA, UCB, UCLA, UP, UV, VHS, W, Y

6. Castell, Robert, *The Villas of the Ancients Illus-*  3
*trated*, London, 1728.
LCP57
A, BaP, BA, BPL, CLS, CW, C, F, HCL, HH, JCB,
JH, LC, LCP, NYM, NYP, PF, UCB, UP, UV, VHS,
W, Y

7. Chambers, Sir William, *Treatise on Civil Archi-*  4
*tecture*, London, 1759 (2nd ed., 1766; others,
1785, 1791, 1825, 1826, 1862).
HCL65, CLS70, Bb73
A, BA, BPL, CW, C, F, HCL, HH, JCB, LC, LCP,
NcD, PF, VHS, W, Y

---

3. Mr. Robert L. Raley, an architect of Newark, Delaware, in a letter dated
October 31, 1961, informed me of a reference to ownership of *Vitruvius Britannicus* in Maryland, in "A Lost Copy-Book of Charles Carroll of Carrollton," ed.
by J. G. D. Paul, *Maryland Historical Magazine*, v. 32, no. 3, September 1937, pp.
193-225. On August 9, 1771, Carroll wrote to his old friend William Graves in
London, "I have not yet received the remaining volumes of *Vitruvius Britannicus*:
Two only have been sent." He again mentioned the problem to Graves on March
17, 1772. On both occasions his London bookseller Payne was mentioned. These
references do not fall within the framework of the present study. They certainly
reflect the peripheral data still to be collected.

8. Copland, H., *A New Book of Ornaments*, London,    4
   1746.
   PH
   W

9. Crunden, John, *The Carpenter's Companion, Con-*    5
   *taining 32 New and Beautiful Designs for All Sorts*
   *of Chinese Railings and Gates*, from the drawings
   of J. H. Morris, Carpenter, and J. Crunden, 1765.[4]
   Bb67
   A, JCB, W

10. Crunden, John, *Convenient and Ornamental Archi-*    5
    *tecture, Consisting of Original Designs for Plans,*
    *Elevations and Sections from the Farm House to*
    *the Most Grand and Magnificent Villa*, London,
    1767 (later eds., 1770, 1785, 1788, 1791, 1797).
    Pb73
    A, BaP, BA, CW, C, HCL, HH, JCB, LC, LCP,
    NYM, NYP, O, SPNEA, UV, VHS, W, Y

---

4. Colvin gives 1770 as the publication date for all of these Crunden books. But there is no doubt about the earlier listings. The copies of no. 9 in the John Carter Brown and Winterthur libraries are dated, whereas the Avery copy is an undated, new edition with thirty-three "new designs" from drawings by J. H. Morris, Carpenter, and J. Crunden. The copies of No. 10 in the Avery Library and the Huntington Library are dated 1767. The Cornell and Boston Athenaeum editions of no. 10 are 1770, the Peabody Institute in Baltimore owns a 1785 edition, and the Huntington one of 1788. Baer lists editions of 1767, 1770, 1791 and 1797. The Winterthur copy of No. 11 is dated 1760, the one at the Huntington 1765.

11. Crunden, John, *The Joyner and Cabinet-Maker's*   5
    *Darling, or Pocket Director*, London, 1760 (another ed. 1765).
    Bb67
    HH, UCB, W

12. Decker, Paul, *Chinese Architecture, Civil and Orna-*   4
    *mental, Adapted to this Climate.* Two Parts.
    London, 1759.
    NYb60, Pb60
    A, BPL, NcD, F, UP, W, Y

13. Dubreuil, Jean, *The Practice of Perspective*, trans-   4
    lated by E. Chambers, 1st ed. 1726.[5]
    LCP41, CLS70
    A, BA, CLS, CW, C, F, HH, JCB, LC, LCP, MB,
    NYP, PF, UV, VHS, W, Y

14. Ferrerio, P., *Palazzi di Roma*, Rome 1655.   1
    B
    A, BPL, C, F, HCL, JH, LC, NYM, NYP, PrP, UP,
    VHS, Y

15. Fréart, Roland, Sieur de Chambray, *A Parallel of*   1
    *the Ancient Architecture with the Modern*, tr. by

---

5. This work appeared in France as *La Perspective Practique*, 2nd ed. Paris, 1651. The first English translation was by R. Pricke in 1672 as *Perspective Practical* (owned by the Free Library of Philadelphia), with a second edition in 1679 and another in 1698. The title was changed in the Chambers translation. Winterthur reports a third edition of 1743, and a fourth of 1765. Additionally, Elizabeth Baer lists editions of 1749, 1782 and 1789.

John Evelyn, London, 1664 (2nd ed. 1707, 3rd 1723, 4th 1733).
Bb1693,[6] NYCC66, CLS70, PH, JW
A, BaP, CW, C, D, F, HCL, HH, JCB, JH, LC, LCP, NcD, NYM, NYP, PF, PrA, PrP, SPNEA, UCB, UCLA, UP, UV, VHS, W, Y

16. Garrett, Daniel, *Designs and Estimates for Farm*    4
    *Houses in the Counties of Yorkshire, Cumberland,*
    *Westmoreland and the Bishoprick of Durham,*
    London, 1747 (3rd ed. 1772).
    NYb62, Pb62, Bb67
    A, JCB, HCL, UCB, UP, VHS, W

17. Gibbs, James, *A Book of Architecture, Containing*    3
    *Designs of Buildings and Ornaments*, London,
    1728 (2nd ed. 1739).
    NYb60, Pb60, CLS70, Bb71, LCP74, Bu, PH, TD
    A, BaP, BA, BPL, CW, C, D, F, HCL, HH, JCB, JH,
    LC, LCP, NcD, NYP, PrA, PrP, RI, SPNEA, UCB,
    UP, UV, VHS, W, Y

18. Gibbs, James, *Rules for Drawing the Several Parts*    3
    *of Architecture*, London, 1732 (2nd ed. 1736, 3rd
    1753).

---

6. The reference in the Samuel Lee book inventory is to "Evenius, Parallel of Architecture," which must be a printer's error for Evelyn's translation of Fréart's *Parellel of the Ancient Architecture with the Modern.* This is the only documented seventeenth-century reference.

Pb54, CLS70, LCP70, PH, TD
A, BaP, BA, CW, C, D, HCL, HH, JCB, LC, LCP, NYM, NcD, O, PrP, RL, SPNEA, UCB, UP, UV, VHS, W, Y

19. Halfpenny, William, *The Art of Sound Building*    2
    *Demonstrated in Geometrical Problems*, London,
    1725.
    B, PH,[7] JW
    A, CW, JCB, UP, UV, VHS, W

20. Halfpenny, William, *The Builder's Pocket Com-*    3
    *panion*, London, 1728 (published under Half-
    penny's pseudonym Michael Hoare; 3rd ed.
    1747).[8]
    Bb61, Pb67
    CW, HH, UP, W

21. Halfpenny, William, *The Country Gentleman's*    4
    *Pocket Companion and Builder's Assistant*, Lon-
    don, 1753 (with John Halfpenny); (2nd ed. 1756).
    NYb60, Pb60
    CW, HCL, LCP, NYM, UP, W, Y

---

7. The Halfpenny books owned by Peter Harrison have been identified by Bridenbaugh. Harrison's inventory in the Connecticut archives lists six books by Halfpenny, four quartos valued at eight, ten, and twelve shillings, an architectural pamphlet valued at six shillings, a "pasteboard" at ten shillings, and a book of architecture at a pound. It is impossible to match these prices and descriptions to specific Halfpenny titles with any certainty. The books themselves are lost.

8. Colvin gives 1747 as the second edition date, but the Huntington Library's third edition is dated 1747.

22. Halfpenny, William, John Halfpenny, Robert    3
Morris, and Thomas Lightoler, *The Modern Build-
er's Assistant or a Concise Epitome of the Whole
System of Architecture*, London, 1742 (later eds.
1747 & 1757).
NYb60, Pb60, PH
A, BPL, CW, F, HH, JCB, JH, NYM, PF, UV, W, Y

23. Halfpenny, William, *A New and Complete System*    4
*of Architecture, Delineated in a Variety of Plans or
Elevations of Designs for Convenient and Deco-
rated Houses*, London, 1749 (2nd ed. 1759, a 1772
edition at Yale).
Pb55, Bb60, PH
A, BaP, BPL, NYSL, UP, VHS, W, Y

24. Halfpenny, William, *New Designs for Chinese*    4
*Temples* (with John Halfpenny), London, 4 parts,
1750-1752.[9]
PH
A, CW, HH, NYM, UP, W, Y

25. Halfpenny, William, *Perspective Made Easy*, Lon-    3
don, 1731.
Bb61 (Architecture in Perspective)
W

26. Halfpenny, William, *Practical Architecture*, Lon-    2
don (1st ed. n.d., 2nd 1724, 5th 1730 (reissued

---

9. William and John Halfpenny also published in 1752 a second edition of
*Rural Architecture in the Chinese Taste*, in four parts. Part one is at Yale bound
with *New Designs*.

1736).[10]
Pb72, PH
A, BaP, CW, HCL, HH, JCB, LCP, MB, NYP, PF,
UP, UV, VHS, W, Y

27. Halfpenny, William, *Rural Architecture in the*   4
    *Gothick Taste*, London, 1752 (with John Half-
    penny).
    NYb60, Pb60, PH
    A, CW, C, F, HCL, HH, JH, LC, LCP, PrP, UP, UV,
    VHS, W, Y

28. Halfpenny, William, *Twelve Beautiful Designs for*   4
    *Farm Houses*, London, 1749 (2nd ed. 1750, others
    1759, 1774).
    Bb60, NYb60, Pb62
    CW, HCL, HH, JCB, LCP, NYP, UP, UV, VHS, W,
    Y

29. Halfpenny, William, *Twenty New Designs of*   4
    *Chinese Lattice and Other Works. . .*, London (first
    edition?, 2nd 1755).[11]
    NYb60, Pb60
    A, W

10. An inscription in the Library Company's copy in Philadelphia reads:
"Isaac Coats bought at Ed Woolleys Vendu this book . . . 1772," according to Mr.
Wolf. The Harvard College Library copy is a 5th ed. dated 1736.

11. Hummel's listing is made from the James Rivington catalogue of 1760
which lists Halfpenny's *Chinese Lattices and Palings*. Colvin includes *Twenty-six
New Designs of Geometric Paling*, published in 1753. The above title was taken
from the Avery's undated copy—it was advertised by Robert Sayer in Yale
University's copy of *Halfpenny's Country Gentleman's Pocket Companion* in the
second edition of 1756. The second edition date is from bibliographical data
supplied by Winterthur.

30. Halfpenny, William, *Useful Architecture*, London,    4
    1752 (later eds. 1755 and 1760).[12]
    LCP57, NYSL58, NYb60, Pb60
    A, CW, JCB, LC, LCP, NYM, UP, VHS, W, Y

31. Hoppus, Edward, *The Gentleman's and Builder's*    3
    *Repository, or Architecture Displayed*, London
    (1st ed. date?, 2nd 1738, 3rd 1748, 4th 1760).[13]
    Pb51, Bb62, NYSL73, Bu, TD
    A, BaP, BA, CW, C, F, HH, JCB, JH, LC, LCP,
    NYM, PrP, SPNEA, UP, VHS, W

32. Hoppus, Edward, *Practical Measuring Made Easy to*    5
    *the Meanest Capacity, by a New Set of Tables*,
    London, 6th ed. 1761.[14]
    Bb65, Bu
    BaP, CW, C, HCL, JCB, LC, UV, VHS, W, Y

33. Johnson, Thomas, *One Hundred and Fifty New*    5
    *Designs, by Thos. Johnson, carver, Consisting of*
    *ceilings, chimney pieces, slab, glass and picture*

---

12. The edition of 1752 is in the Avery, that of 1755 in the Huntington Library and Virginia Historical Society, and 1760 at Yale.

13. Sometimes bound with Salmon's *Builder's Guide*, but by 1760 on its own, at least in the Thomas Dawes' library. Colvin gives a first edition date of 1738, but the Huntington Library's copy is a second edition, dated 1738, also without the *Builder's Guide*. Elizabeth Baer suggests a 1737 publication date. A 1760 edition is in the Virginia Historical Society.

14. The seventh edition of 1765 and thirteenth of 1795 are at the John Carter Brown Library. The eighth edition of 1767 is at Cornell, the ninth of 1771 at the Peabody Institute in Baltimore and the Virginia Historical Society, one of 1790 at Winterthur and 1803 at Yale.

*frames* . . ., London, 1761.
Bu
A, LC, W

34. Jores, J., *A New Book of Iron Work, Containing a*    4
    *Great Variety of Designs, (Useful for Painters,*
    *Cabinet-Makers, Carvers, Smiths, Fillegre-Piercers,*
    *etc.)* . . ., London, 1759.[15]
    NYb62, Pb62, Bb70, PH
    A, BaP, CW, C

35. Keay, Isaac, *Practical Measurer, or Plain Guide to*    2
    *Gentlemen and Builders*, London, 1718 (4th ed.
    1730, 9th 1744, another 1777).[16]
    Bb62, MB
    HCL, JCB, VHS

---

15. This is almost certainly the book which was advertised in New York and Philadelphia as *A New Book of Iron Work* . . ., by J. Jones, in Boston as Jones' *Designs for Iron Work*, and again in Philadelphia as Jones' *Ornamental Designs*. It was identified by Mr. Charles H. Elam, Archivist at the Peale Museum in Baltimore, who recognized it as a book in the collection of the Peabody Institute in Baltimore. A Jones' *Designs* is listed in Thomas Dawes' inventory of books given by his son to the Boston Athenaeum and in Peter Harrison's inventory. In Harrison's inventory "Inigo Jones Architecture" is listed separately, so it is quite likely that Jores' book is meant in the other Jones listing. In the case of Thomas Dawes, we cannot be sure. The volume no longer exists in the Boston Athenaeum. Perhaps the listing should read Jores, or perhaps he owned Ware's or Vardy's *Designs of Inigo Jones*, the latter a re-issue in 1744 of Kent's *Designs of Inigo Jones* of 1727. But the rest of his library does not point to the inclusion of the rarer Palladian volumes, although he did own Campbell's *Vitruvius Britannicus.*

16. Identified by Edwin Wolf II, librarian of the Library Company of Philadelphia. As previously noted, this may have been owned in Virginia by 1728. The tenth edition of 1777 is in the John Carter Brown Library and the Virginia Historical Society.

36. Kent, William, *The Designs of Inigo Jones*, Lon-   3
   don, 1727 (republished 1770).[17]
   PH
   A, BaP, BA, BPL, CLS, CW, C, F, HCL, HH, JH,
   LC, LCP, NcD, NcG, NYP, PF, PrP, SPNEA, UCB,
   UP, USC, UV, VHS, W, Y

37. Langley, Batty and Thomas, *Ancient Masonry,*   3
   *Both in the Theory and in the Practice*, 2 vols.,
   London, 1736.[18]
   ULCP65 (LCP70), Pb73
   A, BaP, BA, BPL, CW, HH, JCB, LC, LCP, PrP, RL,
   UP, UV, VHS, W, Y

38. Langley, Batty, *The Builder's Chest Book, or a*   3
   *Compleat Key to the Five Orders of Columns in*
   *Architecture*, London, 1727 (another ed. 1739).
   NYb60, Pb60, Bb72
   BaP, HH, JCB, LC, NYM, PrP, UV, W

39. Langley, Batty, *The Builder's Compleat Assistant,*   3
   *Being a Library of Arts and Sciences, Absolutely*
   *Necessary to be Understood by Builders and Work-*
   *men in General*, London (1st ed. ?, 4th 1766).[19]
   Pb55, Bb61
   A, CW, C, HCL, LCP, PrA, UP, VHS, W, Y

17. Baer lists other editions of 1735 and 1785.
18. Editions dated 1736 are in the Boston Athenaeum and Winterthur,
although work on this book began in 1732 (see Avery copy preface).
19. An undated second edition is in the Avery Library, a fourth edition dated
1766 is at Cornell. A 1738 edition is listed in the 1768 catalogue of the
Providence Library, now Athenaeum (see Koeper reference, *op. cit.*).

40. Langley, Batty, *The Builder's Director, or Bench-*     4
    *Mate, Containing 500 Examples Engraved on 148*
    *Copper-Plates*, London, 1747 (2nd ed. 1751,
    another 1763).[20]
    Bb65
    A, BaP, CW, HCL, JCB, LC, LCP, NYP, PF, UP,
    UV, VHS, W, Y

41. Langley, Batty and Thomas, *The Builder's Jewel,*     4
    *or the Youth's Instructor, and Workman's Remem-*
    *brancer*, London, 1741 (2nd ed. 1754, 10th 1763,
    11th 1766, 12th 1768; others 1787, 1797 and
    Boston, 1800).
    Pb55, NYb60, Bb65
    A, BaP, BPL, CW, HCL, HH, JCB, LCP, NYM,
    NYP, NYSL, NcD, SPNEA, UP, UV, VHS, W, Y

42. Langley, Batty, *The City and Country Builder's*     4
    *and Workman's Treasury of Designs*, London, 1740
    (with additional plates in 1741, others 1745, 1746,
    1750, and a 4th in 1756).
    Pb54, NYb60, Bb60, Bu, TD, PH(?)[21]

---

20. Colvin gives 1746 as the publication date for this title. However, it is dated 1747 in the Harvard College Library. Colonial Williamsburg reports their title as *The Builder's Benchmate*, dated 1747. The second edition of 1751 is at Harvard and the Avery. An edition of 1763 is in the John Carter Brown Library.

21. Peter Harrison is assumed to have owned Langley's *Treasury* since plate 108 of the 1740 edition was used in his design for the altarpiece in King's Chapel, Boston. The 1740 and 1745 editions are at Winterthur, 1750 at John Carter Brown, and 1756 (the edition owned by Thomas Dawes) at the Boston Athenaeum and the Huntington Library. According to Hummel, 1750 and 1756 editions were owned by members of the Carpenter's Company of Philadelphia.

A, BaP, BA, BPL, CW, C, D, HCL, HH, JCB, LC, LCP, NcD, NYM, PF, PrP, SPNEA, UCB, UP, UV, VHS, W, Y

43. Langley, Batty and Thomas, *Gothick Architecture,*   3
    *Improved by Rules and Proportions*, London, 1742
    (another ed. 1747).[22]
    Bu
    A, BaP, BA, BPL, CW, HCL, HH, JCB, LCP, NYP, PF, PrP, SPNEA, UP, UV, VHS, W, Y

44. Langley, Batty, *Practical Geometry Applied to the*   3
    *Useful Arts of Building, Surveying, Gardening and*
    *Mensuration*, London, 1726 (2nd ed. 1728, 3rd
    1729).
    LCP46
    A, BaP, BA, C, HCL, HH, JCB, LC, LCP, SPNEA, UP, UV, VHS, W, Y

45. Langley, Batty, *The Workman's Golden Rule for*   4
    *Drawing and Working the Five Orders in Archi-*
    *tecture*, London, 1750 (another 1756).[23]
    NYb54, PB60, Bb61
    A, JCB, VHS, W, Y

---

22. According to Colvin, a complete edition of this work was published in 1742, with an essay "On the Principal Ancient Buildings in this Kingdom." The first part was published in 1741. This publication in two parts may explain another reference in Buckland's inventory to "Langley's Essay on Gothic Architecture." Both editions are in the Avery Library.

23. A 1750 edition is in the Virginia Historical Society, and is listed in the RIBA catalogue. 1756 editions are in the Avery, John Carter Brown and Winterthur.

46. LeClerc, Sébastien, *Traité d'Architecture* . . ., Paris,     2
    1714. English translation by Chambers, 1723-
    1724, *A Treatise of Architecture with Remarks
    and Observations . . . for Young People, Who
    Would Apply Themselves to that Art* (later eds.
    1727, 1732).
    Bb61, B,[24] PH
    A, BA, CW, F, JH, JCB, LC, LCP, PF, PrA, PrP,
    SPNEA, UP, UV, VHS, W, Y

47. Leoni, Giacomo, *The Architecture of A. Palladio,*     2
    *in Four Books* . . ., Nicholas Dubois, tr., 2 vols.,
    London, 1715-1716 (2nd ed. 1721, 3rd with
    "Notes and Remarks of Inigo Jones now first taken
    from his original Manuscript in Worcester College
    Oxford" in 1742; French translation in The Hague,
    1726).
    LCP32, Y43, HCL65, B(?)[25]
    A, BaP, BPL, CLS, CW, C, D, F, HCL, HH, JCB,
    JH, LC, LCP, NcD, NYP, NYSL, O, PF, SPNEA,
    UCB, UP, UV, VHS, W, Y

---

24. Mr. Robert Raley of Newark, Delaware, owns the 1714 Paris edition of Le Clerc's *Traité* with the William Byrd bookplate on the inside front cover, and a shelf mark on the inside back cover (cf. letter, *op. cit.*).

25. Byrd's inventory lists a folio and a quarto edition of Palladio. It seems likely that this southern gentleman owned the large Leoni edition and probably Godfrey Richards' *Palladio.* His folio edition of "Alberti's Architecture" was probably also Leoni's, as is suggested in the following listing. The tenth architectural book in Byrd's library is listed as *Principes l'Architecture,* and is unidentified.

48. Leoni, Giacomo, *The Architecture of L. Alberti*, 3    3
    vols., 1726 (later eds. 1739 and 1755).
    ULCP65 (LCP70), B(?)
    A, BA, BPL, CW, C, F, HH, JH, LCP, NcD, UP,
    UV, VHS, W, Y

49. Leybourn, William, *The Mirror of Architecture or*    1
    *the Ground Rules of the Art of Building according*
    *to Vincenzo Scamozzi, with the Description and*
    *Use of a Joynt Rule by John Brown, Whereunto is*
    *Added a Compendium of the Art of Building,*
    London, 1669 (revised and enlarged 1676, 4th ed.
    1700, 5th 1708, others 1721, 1734, 1768).
    Bb54, B
    A, BA, CW, C, D, JH, JCB, LC, LCP, NYM, PrA,
    UCB, UCLA, UP, VHS, W, Y

50. Lightoler, Thomas, *The Gentleman's and Farmer's*    5
    *Architect, . . . Being Correct Plans and Elevations*
    *of Parsonage and Farm Houses . . .*, London, 1762
    (another ed. 1764).
    Bu
    BaP, BA, CW, HCL, JCB, UP, UV, VHS, W, Y

51. Miller, John, *Andrea Palladio's Elements of Archi-*    4
    *tecture, Restored to its Original Perfection . . .*
    *with a Geometrical Explanation of its True Prin-*
    *ciples of Perspective*, London, ca. 1748 (another
    ed. 1759).
    Pb63
    F, JCB, JH

52. Morris, Robert, *Architecture Improved in a Collec-*    4
    *tion of Modern, Elegant and Useful Designs,*
    London, 1755.
    NYb60, Pb60, Bb61, Bu, PH
    CW, HCL, NYP, UP, W, Y

53. Morris, Robert, *Lectures on Architecture, Con-*    3
    *sisting of Rules Founded upon Harmonick and*
    *Arithmetical Proportions in Building,* London,
    1734-1736 (2nd ed. 1759).
    Bb73, PH(?)[26]
    A, CLS, CW, UCB, UV, VHS, W, Y

54. Morris, Robert, *Essay in Defence of Ancient Archi-*    3
    *tecture, or a Parallel of the Ancient Buildings with*
    *the Modern, Shewing the Beauty and Harmony of*
    *the Former, and the Irregularity of the Latter,*
    London, 1728.
    PH
    A, CW, HH, NYSL, UV, W

55. Morris, Robert, *Select Architecture, Being Regular*    4
    *Designs of Plans, and Elevations, Well Suited to*

---

26. This may be the *Harmony of Building* which is listed in Harrison's
inventory. Mr. Lawrence Kocher, according to the Colonial Williamsburg librarian,
considered that the *Essay on Harmony as It Relates Chiefly to Situation and
Building* was wrongly attributed to John Gwynn, and was in fact Morris's. There
are three other Morris references in the Harrison inventory which cannot be
firmly identified. The prices given are almost certainly inaccurate and there are
not even short titles, so that identification is risky. In the absence of further
evidence, Bridenbaugh's identifications have been used.

65

*Both Town and Country...*, London, 1755
(another ed. 1757).[27]
NYb60, Pb60, PH
A, CW, HCL, JCB, UV, VHS, W, Y

56.  Moxon, Joseph, *Practical Perspective, or Perspective Made Easie*, London, 1670.[28]     1
B
A, BPL, F, HCL, HH, JH, JCB, NYM, NYP, UCLA, VHS, W

57.  Moxon, Joseph, *The Theory and Practice of Architecture; or Vitruvius and Vignola Abridg'd*, London, 5th ed. 1703.[29]     2
LL51
A, JH, JCB, LCP, UCLA, W

58.  Neve, Richard, *City and Country Purchaser's and Builder's Dictionary*, London, 1703 (2nd ed. 1726, 3rd 1736).     2
Y43, LL51, ALCP65, ULCP65 (LCP70)
A, BaP, BA, CW, C, HCL, HH, JCB, LC, LCP, UP, UV, VHS, W, Y

---

27. Colvin dates this 1755 and gives a second edition date of 1759. A 1755 edition is in the Virginia Historical Society, and the Avery copy is dated 1757.

28. Mr. Wolf has informed me that this was erroneously reported as being present in the Library Company in 1770.

29. Moxon also published his Barozzio translation separately as *Vignola: or the Compleat Architect*. The Vitruvius is listed in the R.I.B.A. catalogue as by "Mr. Perrault." The fifth edition listed is in the Avery.

59. Oakley, Edward, *Every Man a Complete Builder, or*   3
    *Easy Rules and Proportions for Drawing and Work-*
    *ing the Several Parts of Architecture,* London,
    1738 (later eds. 1766, 1774).
    Bb67
    Bap, LC, NYM, W, Y

60. Oakley, Edward, *The Magazine of Architecture,*   3
    *Perspective and Sculpture,* London, 1730 (another
    ed. 1733).
    RL50
    BaP, RL, VHS, W, Y

61. Over, Charles, *Ornamental Architecture in the*   4
    *Gothic, Chinese and Modern Taste,* London, 1758.
    NYb60, Pb60
    A, HH, NYM, NYP, UCB, UP, VHS, W, Y

62. Overton, Thomas Collins, *The Temple Builder's*   5
    *Most Useful Companion, Being . . . Fifty New . . .*
    *Designs for Pleasure and Recreation,* London,
    1766.
    PH[30]
    A, HH, JCB, LC, LCP, NYP, UCB, UP, VHS, W, Y

63. Pain, William, *The Builder's Companion . . . [in-*   4
    *cludes] the figure, description and use of a new-*
    *invented joint-rule,* London, 1758 (2nd ed. 1762,
    3rd 1769).

---

30. Bridenbaugh thought this was the "Overt arch quarto" referred to in the Harrison inventory, but it might also have been Over.

Bb60, NYb60, Pb60, CCM62, CLS70, TD, PH
A, BaP, BA, BPL, CW, HCL, JCB, LCP, NYM, PF,
PrA, SPNEA, UP, UV, VHS, W, Y

64. Pain, William, *The Builder's Pocket Treasure, or,*     5
*Palladio Delineated and Explained*, London, 1763
(2nd ed. 1766, others 1783 and Boston, 1794).
Bb71
A, BPL, CW, HCL, HH, JCB, UCB, W, Y

65. Palladio, Andrea, *I Quattro Libri dell'Architettura*,     1
Venice, 1570 (later eds. 1581, 1601, 1616, 1642,
1711).
HCL65 (eds. of 1570 and 1581)
A, BaP, BA, BPL, CW, D, F, HCL, JH, LC, LCP,
NYP, NcC, O, UP, UV, Y

66. Perrault, Claude, *Treatise of the Five Orders of*     1
*Columns in Architecture*, 1st French edition, Paris,
1683, tr. by John James, London, 1708 (2nd ed.
1722).
HCL23, ULCP54 (LCP70), LL65 (Paris, 1693), JW
A, BA, CW, C, F, HCL, HH, JCB, JH, LC, LCP,
NYM, NYP, NYSL, NcD, PrP, UP, UV, VHS, W, Y

67. Price, Francis, *The British Carpenter, or a Treatise*     3
*on Carpentry*, London, 1733 (2nd ed. 1735, 3rd
1753, another 1759, 5th 1765, 6th 1768).
LCP39, RL50, ULCP53, PB54, NYb60, BB61,
CCM71
A, BaP, BA, CW, C, D, HH, JCB, LC, LCP, RL, UP,
UV, VHS, W, Y

68. Ralph, James, *Critical Review of the Publick Build-*    3
*ings, Statues and Ornaments in and about London*
*and Westminster*, London, 1734.
RL64
A, BaP, BA, CW, HCL, HH, JCB, LCP, NYM, RL,
UCLA, UV, Y

69. Richards, Godfrey, tr., *The First Book of Archi-*    1
*tecture by Andrea Palladio . . . with an Appendix*
*Touching Doors and Windows*, by Pr. Le Muet,
Architect to the French King, London, 1663 (2nd
ed. 1668, 3rd 1676, 6th 1700, 7th 1708, 8th 1716,
9th 1721, 11th 1729, 12th 1773).[31]
B(?), LL65, TD
A, BA, BPL, CW, C, F, HH, JCB, LCP, NcD, NcRS,
NYP, SPNEA, UCLA, UV, VHS, W

70. Riou, Stephen, *Short Principles for the Architec-*    5
*ture of Stone Bridges, with Practical Observations*
. . ., London, 1748 (another ed. 1760).[32]
Bb73, TD
A, BA, LC, LCP, RL, W

---

31. Fiske Kimball was the original source for the edition dates of this book in *Domestic Architecture of the American Colonies and of the Early Republic* (New York, 1922), p. 58, except for the second and third editions. A second edition is in the library of the Essex Institute, Salem, inscribed "Tomas Pars"; a third edition is in the Williams Andrews Clark Memorial Library of the University of California, Los Angeles. Additionally, the John Carter Brown Library and Winterthur have reported an eighth edition of 1716, and the Boston Athenaeum, Cornell and the New York Public Library an eleventh of 1729.

32. Bound with Swan's *Upwards of One Hundred and Fifty New Designs for Chimney Pieces . . .*, in the Dawes Library at the Boston Athenaeum.

71. Rusconi, Giovanni, *Della Architettura*, Venice,　1
1590 (2nd ed. 1660).
HCL65 (Venice 1590)
A, BaP, Ba, F, HCL, JH, NYM, NYP, UP, Y

72. Salmon, William, *The Builder's Guide and Gentle-*　4
*man and Trader's Assistant*, London, 1736.[33]
Bb54, NYb60, Pb60
A, JCB, UP, UV, VHS, W

73. Salmon, William, *The Country Builder's Estimator*　3
*or the Architect's Companion*, London, 1736 (2nd
ed. by Hoppus 1737, 3rd 1746, 4th 1752, 5th
1755, 7th 1759, 8th by J. Green 1770, 9th 1774).
NYb60, Pb60, Bb73
A, BaP, CW, F, HCL, JCB, JH, UP, VHS, W

74. Salmon, William, *The London and Country*　4
*Builder's Vade Mecum: or the Complete and Uni-*
*versal Estimator*, London, 1745 (2nd ed. 1748, 3rd
1755, 4th 1760).
NYb55, Pb60, Bb61, WSJ, JW
A, CW, HCL, HH, JCB, LCP, NYM, UP, VHS, W, Y

75. Salmon, William, *Palladio Londinensis, or, the Lon-*　3
*don Art of Building*, London, 1734 (2nd ed. 1738,

---

33. Apparently this was advertised separately, although Colvin notes that it
was published at the end of Hoppus' *Gentleman's Repository* in 1748. The Avery
and John Carter Brown copies are dated 1736.

3rd 1748, others 1762, 7th of 1767, and 1773).[34]
Pb51, NYb60, Bb61, RL64, NH65, CLS70,
LCP70, Bu, PH, TD
A, BaP, BA, CW, C, HCL, HH, JCB, LC, LCP, NYP,
PF, RL, SPNEA, UP, UV, VHS, W, Y

76. Serlio, Sebastiano, *Tutte L'Opera d'Architettura*,   1
Venice, 1584 (2nd ed. 1600, 3rd 1619, others
1663, 1684).
HCL65 (Venice 1684)
A, BA, C, F, HCL, HH, JH, NYP, NcD, RL, RI,
UP, UV, VHS, W, Y

77. *Several Prospects of the Most Noted Buildings in*   2
*London*, London, 1724.
LCP70
A, HH, LC, LCP

78. Smith, James, *The Carpenter's Companion*, Lon-   3
don, 1733.[35]
RL64
A, JCB, RL, UP, VHS, W, Y

79. Swan, Abraham, *The British Architect, or, the*   4
*Builder's Treasury of Staircases*, London, 1745

---

34. Beginning with the third edition of 1748 "with great Alterations and
Improvements by E. Hoppus" (from the Dawes copy in the Boston Athenaeum).
A second edition of 1738 has been reported by Winterthur and editions of 1762,
1767 and 1773. The Free Library of Philadelphia has reported a seventh edition
of 1767.

35. I am indebted to Mr. Wolf for identification of this work and for the full
title of number 77.

(later eds. 1748, 1750, 1758, Philadelphia 1775, Boston 1794).
Pb60, NYb60, Bb63, CCM65, LCP75, Bu, PH
A, BaP, BA, BPL, CW, C, F, HCL, HH, JCB, JH, LC, LCP, NcD, NYM, NYP, NYSL, PF, UCB, UP, USC, UV, VHS, W, Y

80. Swan, Abraham, *A Collection of Designs in Archi-    4
tecture*, 2 vols., London, 1757.
Pb62, ALCP65, ULCP65 (LCP70), Bb72, Bu,[36]
PH
A, BaP, BA, BPL, CW, HCL, HH, JCB, LC, LCP, NcD, NYP, PF, SPNEA, UCB, UCLA, UP, VHS, W, Y

81. Swan, Abraham, *Designs in Carpentry*, London,    4
1759 (another version in 1768 under title *The Carpenter's Complete Instructor in Several Hundred Designs*).[37]
Pb73, Bu, TD, PH
A, BA, JCB, W, Y

36. Buckland's inventory lists Swan's *"British Treasury"* (no. 79) and Swan's *"Architect,"* almost certainly this other major publication.

37. Hummel noted that Philadelphia bookseller David Hall ordered two copies of Swan's *Designs in Carpentry* in 1755–before the work listed here was published. These two references are not included in the total number of references to this work.

82. Swan, Abraham, *Upwards of One Hundred and Fifty New Designs for Chimney Pieces*, London, 1768.[38]    5
    Bb72, TD
    A, BA, UP, VHS, W, Y

83. Vitruvius, *De Architettura*, 1st printed Venice, 1483.    1
    HCL65 (Venice 1584)
    CLS70 Amsterdam 1649 (with Wotton's *Elements*)
    LL51 Amsterdam 1649 (with Wotton's *Elements*)
    A, BaP, BA, CLS, CW, C, D, F, HCL, HH, JCB, JH, LC, LCP, NcD, NYM, NYP, PF, UCB, UP, UV, VHS, Y

84. Ware, Isaac, *A Complete Body of Architecture*, 2 vols., London, 1756 (later ed. 1767).[39]    5
    Bb60, NYb61, Pb61, LCP64, Bu, PH
    A, BaP, BA, CW, C, D, F, HCL, HH, JCB, JH, LC, LCP, NcD, NYM, NYP, PF, PrA, RL, SPNEA, UCB, UP, UV, VHS, W, Y

---

38. Swan's *Designs for Chimneys* available in 1772 in Boston at Henry Knox's "London Book-Store" may have been this title or another Swan publication, *Designs for Chimnies and the Proportion They Bear to Their Respective Rooms*, to which Colvin gives a publication date of 1765 (a copy at Yale is undated, as is one in the John Carter Brown Library). Copies of the listed title in the Boston Athenaeum and Winterthur are dated 1768.

39. Colvin suggests a first edition date of 1735 for this work, but no edition earlier than 1756 has been reported. Baer lists 1757, 1758 and 1767. Winterthur and the Avery own editions of 1756 and 1767, the Free Library of Philadelphia one of 1767.

85. Ware, Isaac, *Designs of Inigo Jones and Others*,   3
London, 1735 (later eds. 1743, 1756).
Pb54, PH
A, BaP, BA, CLS, CW, C, HCL, HH, JCB, JH, LC,
LCP, NcD, NYM, O, PrP, UP, UV, VHS, W, Y

86. Ware, Isaac, *The Four Books of Andrea Palladio's*   3
*Architecture* ..., London, 1738 (another ed.
1755).
ULCP54 (LCP70), Bb60, NYb60, RL64, CLS70
A, BaP, BA, CW, JCB, JH, LCP, NYSL, PF, PrP,
RL, UCLA, UP, UV, VHS, W

87. Ware, Isaac, William Kent and Thomas Ripley, *The*   3
*Plans . . . of Houghton in Norfolk*, . . . Delineated
by I. Ware and W. Kent . . ., London, 1735 (a later
ed. 1760).
PH
A, BaP, BA, CW, HCL, HH, JCB, LCP, NYM, NYP,
UP, VHS, W, Y

# Additional Listings

101. Barker, John, *The Measurer's Guide*, London,    1
   1692.[40]
   PCC (c. 1700)

102. Darling, John, *The Carpenters Rule Made Easie.*    1
   *Or, the Art of Measuring Superficies and Solids; as*
   *Timber, Stone, Board, Glasse, and the Like ...*
   *Performed by Certain Tables ...,* Worcester,
   1658.[41]
   MB

103. Fletcher, Abraham, *The Universal Measurer and*    4
   *Mechanic*, two parts, Whitehaven, 1752-1753
   (another edition, London, 1762; 3rd 1766).[41]
   Pb73
   LCP

---

40. This title occurs in the Christ Church, Philadelphia, library, records for which are now in the Library Company of Philadelphia. It was identified by Edwin Wolf II, whose reference was Edward Arber, ed., *The Term Catalogues*, London, 1903-1906, II, pp. 410-411. Mr. Wolf thinks that the library, sent to Christ Church by Dr. Thomas Bray, reached Philadelphia in 1700 (*The Annual Report of the Library Company of Philadelphia for the Year 1966*, "Report of the Librarian," p. 17).

41. Numbers 102 through 105 and 112 have been identified only through the catalogue of the British Museum. Mr. Wolf of the Library Company of Philadelphia notes that no. 103 in the Library Company's collection is *The Universal Measurer, and Mechanic*, in three parts, London, 1766. It is described as a second edition, but Mr. Wolf agrees that it is actually the third.

104. Foster, —, *Art of Measuring* (perhaps *Posthuma*      1
     *Fosteri: the Description of a Ruler*, London,
     1652).⁴¹
     MB
     HH

105. Fournier, Daniel, *A Treatise of the Theory and*      5
     *Practice of Perspective. Wherein the Principles . . .*
     *as Laid Down by Dr. B. Taylor are Explained, by*
     *means of Moveable Schemes, etc.,* London, 1761 (a
     second edition, enlarged, 1652).⁴¹
     Pb73
     W (1761 ed.)

106. Hawney, William, *The Compleat Measurer. . .,* Lon-      2
     don, 1717 (third ed. 1729, fifth and eighth in
     Dublin in 1730 and 1785, sixth in London 1748,
     eleventh 1763, twelfth 1766, thirteenth 1769, new
     edition corrected 1798, another 1805, 1809).⁴²
     Bb34, Pb44, WSJ, HCL65
     A, HH, LCP

107. Labelye, Charles, *A Description of Westminster*      4
     *Bridge*, London, 1751.⁴³
     Bb73
     HH, LCP

---

42. Eight references, from 1734 in Boston to 1773 in Philadelphia, were
found for this important book.

43. Two preliminary accounts of methods of building were published in 1739
and 1743. They are listed in the British Museum catalogue, and the 1743 and
1751 volumes are in the Huntington Library.

108. Langley, Batty, *Carpenter's Companion.*[44]   ?
Bb66

109. Langley, Batty, *The London Prices of Bricklayer's*   4
*Materials and Works . . . Justly Ascertained . . .,*
London, 1748. (Another ed. 1750).
Bb72
A, HH, W

110. LeClerc, Sébastien, *Practical Geometry . . . Trans-*   2
*lated from the French of S. LeClerc* (the third
edition . . . with copperplates, . . . T. Bowles, London 1727, a sixth edition 1742).[45]
CLS70
HH, LCP

111. Mandey, Venterus, *Mellificium Mensionis: or, the*   1
*Marrow of Measuring,* London, 1682 (fourth ed.
1727).
Bb34
HH, LCP

112. Miles, Thomas, *The Concise Practical Measurer; or,*   3
*a Plain Guide to Gentlemen and Builders* (second
ed. London, 1740).[41]
Bb72
LCP

44. I have been unable to identify this title.
45. Richard Neve in his preface to the *City and Country Purchaser's and Builder's Dictionary* cites LeClerc as reducing the studies necessary for the architect — Designing, Geometry, Arithmetick, Stone-cutting, Perspective, Mechanicks, Levelling, and Hydraulicks. Neve includes surveying in his *Builder's Dictionary*. It does not appear in the *Builder's Dictionary* of 1734 (no. 4 on this list).

113. Noble, Edward, *The Elements of Linear Perspec-* 5
*tive, Demonstrated by Geometrical Principles*, London, 1771.[46]
Bb72
HH, LCP, W

114. Partridge, Seth, *The Description and Use of an* 1
*Instrument Called the Double Scale of Proportion*
. . ., London, 1671 (other eds. 1685, 1692).
Bb34
HH

115. Pozzo, Andrea, *Rules and Examples of Perspective* 1
*Proper for Painters and Architects, etc. In English*
*and Latin* . . . By Mr. John James . . ., London,
1707.[47]
JW
A, BA, C, D, LC, LCP, NYP, NcD, PF, UP, VHS, W

116. Riou, Stephen, *The Grecian Orders of Architec-* 5
*ture, Delineated and Explained from the Antiqui-*
*ties of Athens: also the Parallels of the Orders of*

---

46. This title also occurs in a Dixon and Hunter advertisement of November
25, 1775, in the *Virginia Gazette*, mentioned in "Books in Williamsburg," in the
*William and Mary Quarterly*, v. 15, 1906, pp. 100-113; and in a 1772 Knox bill in
the Massachusetts Historical Society. It is dedicated to "Sir Joshua Reynolds,
Knt., President of the Royal Academy of Painting, Sculpture and Architecture
and Fellow of the Royal Society." It was printed for T. Davies, "Bookseller to the
Royal Academy."
47. This book was owned by Joseph Wragg of Charleston, who died c.
1751-1753, according to Beatrice Ravenel in *Architects of Charleston*, 1945. The
Library Company of Philadelphia owns the Rome edition of 1741, *Perspectiva*
*Pictorum.*

*Palladio, Scamozzi and Vignola . . .*, London, 1768.
Bb73[48]
LCP, W

117. Sturmy, —, *Architecture, Staticks, Mechanicks,*    ?
*Opticks, Catoptricks, Dioptricks and Astronomy.*[49]
Pb44

118. Taylor, Brook, *Linear Perspective: or, a New*    2
*Method of Representing Justly All Manner of
Objects. . .*, London, 1715 (other eds. 1719, 1749;
presented by J. J. Kirby, 1754, 1755, 1768).
Pb73
HH, LCP, W

119. Wotton, Sir Henry, *The Elements of Architecture,*    1
*Collected . . . from the Best Authors and Ex-
amples*, London, 1624 (*The Ground-rules . . .
Abridged*, 1686).[50]
HCL23, LL51, CLS70
A, BA, CLS, HCL, HH, JCB, LCP, NYP, PrA, UV,
VHS, W

---

48. This title appears three times in Knox documents in the seventies.

49. I have been unable to track down this book advertised by Benjamin Franklin in Philadelphia.

50. Wotton's *Elements* was apt to be included with more precise studies, such as the 1649 Amsterdam (Latin) edition of Vitruvius and the English edition of Perrault available at Harvard in 1723.